# Instant
# One-Pot
# Cooking

Paré • Pirk • Darcy

Distributed by
**Canada Book Distributors**
www.canadabookdistributors.com
www.companyscoming.com
Tel: 1-800-661-9017

**Library and Archives Canada Cataloguing in Publication**

Paré, Jean, author
  Instant one-pot cooking / Jean Paré, Wendy Pirk and James Darcy.

Includes index.
Issued in print and electronic formats.
ISBN 978-1-77207-039-2 (softcover).--ISBN 978-1-77207-040-8 (EPUB)
  1. Pressure cooking. 2. Cookbooks. I. Darcy, James, author
II. Title.

TX840.P7P37 2018          641.5'87          C2018-902766-5
                                             C2018-902824-6

All inside photos by Company's Coming except: from Sandy Wheatherall, 13, 17, 19, 22, 24, 26, 33, 39, 43, 45, 51, 53, 55, 59, 75, 83, 93, 97, 99, 117, 119, 127. From Thinkstock: 3sbworld, 34–35; a_namenko, 88; anandaBGD, 115; Anna_Shepulova, 131; bhofack2, 57, 145; chas53, 31; cheche22, 73; Chiyacat, 47; cobraphoto, 11, 125; Danler, 153; Elena_Danileiko, 85; furo_felix, 71; Gilles_Paire, 8; luknaja, 29; marekuliasz, 142–143; Mariha-kitchen, 79, 149; martinturzak, 137; mikafotostok, 87; OksanaKiian, 5, 65; ozgurcoskun, 128; PhotoBylove, 49; rez-art, 147; Sarsmis, 77; stockphoto24, 81; sutsaiy, 109; tacar 59; TLRaney, 48; Yelena Yemchuk, 67, 154; yuryRumovsky, 62, 76; zefirchik06, 95.

We acknowledge the financial support of the Government of Canada.
Nous reconnaissons l'appui financier du gouvernement du Canada.

Funded by the Government of Canada
Financé par le gouvernement du Canada   |   Canadä

PC: 38-4

# Table of Contents

# The Jean Paré Story

Jean Paré (pronounced "jeen PAIR-ee") grew up understanding that the combination of family, friends and home cooking is the best recipe for a good life. When Jean left home, she took with her a love of cooking, many family recipes and an intriguing desire to read cookbooks as if they were novels!

**"Never share a recipe you wouldn't use yourself."**

When her four children had all reached school age, Jean volunteered to cater the 50th anniversary celebration of the Vermilion School of Agriculture, now Lakeland College, in Alberta, Canada. Working from her home, Jean prepared a dinner for more than 1,000 people and from there launched a flourishing catering operation that continued for more than 18 years.

As requests for her recipes increased, Jean was often asked, "Why don't you write a cookbook?" The release of *150 Delicious Squares* on April 14, 1981, marked the debut of what would soon turn into one of the world's most popular cookbook series.

Company's Coming cookbooks are distributed in Canada, the United States, Australia and other world markets. Bestsellers many times over in English, Company's Coming cookbooks have also been published in French and Spanish.

Familiar and trusted in home kitchens around the world, Company's Coming cookbooks are offered in a variety of formats. Highly regarded as kitchen workbooks, the softcover Original Series, with its lay-flat plastic comb binding, is still a favourite among home cooks.

Jean Paré's approach to cooking has always called for quick and easy recipes using everyday ingredients. That view served her well, and the tradition continues in the Practical Gourmet series.

Jean's Golden Rule of Cooking is: Never share a recipe you wouldn't use yourself. It's an approach that has worked—millions of times over!

# Introduction

Multi-cookers are taking the world by storm, and with good reason. Counter space is at a premium in many kitchens, and with the multi-cooker you get a pressure cooker, slow cooker, rice cooker, steamer and yogurt maker all in one handy appliance.

Space-saving qualities aside, the real selling point of the multi-cooker is its versatility. The **pressure cooker function** allows you to get many delicious meals to the table in much less time than they would take in the oven or slow cooker, and with unmatched convenience. There is no need to fuss with or check on the dish as it cooks; just set it up and walk away until the timer lets you know that your food is ready.

The **slow cooker function** is perfect for times when you want to come home to a meal that is ready for the table. Just set it up before you leave in the morning so it can be ready by the time you get home.

Thanks to the **sauté function**, the multi-cooker is truly a one-pot cooking experience. No need to use a frying pan to caramelize onions or sear meat before adding it to the pressure or slow cooker. Just toss your ingredients into the inner pot, hit the sauté function and take care of business right there. You can also use the sauté function to simmer soups and reduce sauces.

The **rice cooker function** makes perfect fluffy rice, and with the **yogurt function** you can make rich, creamy yogurt with almost no effort on your part. The **steamer function** turns out some of the best corn on the cob you will ever taste, and you can even try your hand at sous vide cooking. Really, is there anything the multi-cooker cannot do?

Well, actually, there is.

As amazing as the multi-cooker is, it is not a miracle pot. We understand how much people love their multi-cookers. It's easy to get caught up in the excitement of your new favourite appliance try to mould every dish into a pressure-cooker recipe, but the truth is there are times when you are best off giving the multi-pot a pass and reaching for a frying pan or the oven instead.

For some foods, using the multi-cooker is more trouble than it's worth. It doesn't make sense to pull out the multi-pot to cook a stir-fry that you could whip up faster on the stovetop. As a general rule, if you can prepare a dish in a frying pan in 20 minutes or less, go for that option.

Pressure cooker times refer to how long the food takes to cook under pressure; they do not factor in how long the cooker takes to build and release pressure. Even if the actual cooking time is less in the pressure cooker, the overall time may be longer.

And sometimes, the multi-pot is just not the right tool. You wouldn't use a screwdriver when the task at hand requires a hammer, and if you did you'd most likely be disappointed with the results. The same can be said for the multi-cooker. Some dishes, such as breaded foods and most types of fish, seafood and delicate vegetables, do not fare well under pressure. Choose another cooking method.

Another limitation of the multi-cooker is that you can't adjust your recipe as you go along. There is no opportunity to taste and adjust seasonings, and you can't check for doneness during the cooking process. Basically, once the cooking cycle is finished, you get what you get.

If you keep these limitations in mind, you are destined to have many happy days preparing delicious meals with your multi-cooker!

# Pressure Cooking Chart

As you travel the path to multi-cooker mastery and start adjusting your own recipes for your cooker, use the following chart to help you figure out how long to cook your dishes. Remember that these times are just guidelines; adjust them according to your own preferences.

| Type | Cooking Time (minutes) |
|------|------------------------|
| **Meat** | |
| Beef, stew meat | 15–20 |
| Braising/simmering beef: small chunks | 25–30 |
| Braising/simmering beef: whole | 35–40 |
| Beef, ribs | 25–30 |
| Beef, shanks | 25–30 |
| Chicken, breasts | 8–10 |
| Chicken, legs | 10–15 |
| Chicken, whole | 20–25 |
| Ham, picnic shoulder | 25–30 |
| Ham, shank or butt portion | 9–12 |
| Pork, butt/shoulder roast | 15–20 |
| Pork, loin roast | 55–60 |
| Pork, ribs | 20–25 |
| Lamb, leg | 35–45 |
| Lamb, stew meat | 10–15 |
| Turkey, boneless breasts | 15–20 |
| Turkey, drumsticks | 15–20 |
| **Dried Beans, Legumes and Lentils** | |
| Adzuki beans | 20–25 |
| Black beans | 20–30 |
| Black-eyed peas | 20–25 |
| Cannellini beans | 20–25 |
| Chickpeas/garbanzo beans | 35–40 |
| Great Northern beans | 20–25 |
| Kidney beans, red | 20–25 |
| Kidney beans, white | 35–40 |
| Lentils, French green | 15–20 |
| Lentils, red | 15–18 |
| Lentils, yellow, split | 15–18 |
| Lima beans | 20–25 |
| Navy beans | 25–30 |
| Pinto beans | 25–30 |

| Type | Cooking Time (minutes) |
|------|------------------------|
| **Vegetables** | |
| Artickoke, hearts | 4–5 |
| Asparagus, whole or cut | 1–2 |
| Beans, green/yellow or wax, whole ends trimmed | 1–2 |
| Beets, large, whole | 20–25 |
| Beets, small whole | 11–13 |
| Brussels sprouts, whole | 3–4 |
| Cabbage, red or green, wedges | 3–4 |
| Carrots, sliced or shredded | 1–2 |
| Carrots, whole or chunks | 2–3 |
| Celery, chunks | 2–3 |
| Corn, kernels | 1–2 |
| Corn, on the cob | 3–4 |
| Leeks | 2–4 |
| Parsnips, chunks | 2–4 |
| Peas, green | 1–2 |
| Peas, snow pea or sugar pea | 1–2 |
| Potatoes, cubed | 7–9 |
| Potatoes, whole, baby | 10–12 |
| Potatoes, whole, large | 12–15 |
| Pumpkin, large slices or chunks | 8–10 |
| Pumpkin, small slices or chunks | 4–5 |
| Rutabaga, chunks | 4–6 |
| Rutabaga, slices | 3–2 |
| Squash, acorn, slices or chunks | 6–7 |
| Squash, butternut, slices or chunks | 8–10 |
| Sweet potato, cubed | 7–9 |
| Sweet potato, whole, large | 12–15 |
| Sweet potato, whole, small | 10–12 |

# The Pressure Cooker Demystified

The words "pressure cooker" for many conjure up visions of horrible injuries caused by explosions of steam and scorching hot liquid. Understandably, many home cooks who have grown up hearing these horror stories are too intimidated by the pressure cooker to ever consider using one.

Thankfully, with the multi-cooker you can lay those fears to rest. These handy appliances, regardless of the brand you chose, are created with fail-safe technology and sensors that ensure the appliance is as safe and user-friendly as your microwave or toaster.

However, as with all technology, there are a few things you need to know about the pressure cooker and how it works to ensure that you get the most out of your soon-to-be-favourite appliance.

First, how it works. As its name suggests, a pressure cooker uses pressure to bring up the temperature inside the pot so that food cooks faster. Water boiling away in a pot on a stovetop cannot get any hotter than 212°F (100°C) because at that point the water turns into water vapour (i.e. steam). With the pressure cooker, however, the lid is sealed so that the water vapour cannot escape; the trapped vapour bounces around inside the pot, raising the pressure and therefore the temperature.

Altitude affects how quickly your multi-cooker can build pressure and therefore how long it takes to cook your food. The recipes in this book were developed for sea level up to 2000 feet (610 metres); if you live at a higher altitude, you will need to adjust the cooking times. As a general rule, you should increase cooking time by 5 percent for every 1000 feet (305 metres) you live above 2000 feet (610 metres) above sea level.

Once the pressure cooking cycle is complete, the pressure in the inner pot must be released. Knowing what kind of pressure release to use for your dish is a key component of mastering the multi-cooker. For a quick release, you manually turn the pressure release valve, which allows the steam to escape quickly through the valve. The food stops cooking as soon as the pressure is completely released. We suggest covering the pressure vent with a tea towel to prevent blasting steam all over your cupboards; also, if you are doing a quick release of a recipe with a really full pot, liquid such as tomato sauce or broth can be ejected through the vent and splatter the counter and surrounding area, including you.

With a natural release, the steam and pressure dissipate naturally once the cooking cycle has ended. Depending on the amount of food in the pot, this can take upwards of twenty minutes, and the food in the pot continues to cook as the steam and pressure drop. Recipes that call for a natural release have factored the time it takes for the pressure to release into the cooking time, so do not do a quick release on a recipe that calls for a natural release or your food might be undercooked.

## Tips for Success

- The multi-cooker needs at least 1 cup (250 mL) of liquid, or it will not build up enough pressure to cook your food.

- Do not overfill your inner pot. It should never be more than two-thirds full, and when cooking foods that expand or foam, such as legumes, rice or other grains, it should be only half full.

- When cooking frozen meat, add about 50 percent more cooking time.

- The cooking time does not change based on the quantity of food you are cooking, so if, for example, you are doubling a recipe, you do not need to increase the cooking time. However, quantity does affect the time it takes for the cooker to build and release pressure. The fuller the pot, the longer it will take the multi-cooker to reach full pressure and start the cooking cycle, and then to naturally release the pressure once the cycle is complete.

# French Onion Soup

*A chic Parisian would never dream of spending hours slaving over a hot stove, so why should you? Let your multi-cooker do most of the work for you.*

| | | |
|---|---|---|
| Butter (or hard margarine), melted | 2 tbsp. | 30 mL |
| Olive (or cooking) oil | 2 tbsp. | 30 mL |
| Thinly sliced onion | 5 cups | 1.25 L |
| Dried thyme | 1/2 tsp. | 2 mL |
| Beef stock | 8 cups | 2 L |
| Dry red wine | 1/4 cup | 60 mL |
| Salt, just a pinch (optional) | | |
| Baguette bread slices, about 1 inch (2.5 mm) thick | 12 | 12 |
| Grated Gruyére (or mozzarella) cheese | 3/4 cup | 175 mL |

With sauté function, heat butter and olive oil in inner pot on medium. Add onion and stir until well coated. Sprinkle with thyme. Cook, stirring, for about 5 minutes until onion softens. Turn off sauté function. Cover with lid and seal. Select pressure cooker function. Cook on high pressure for 20 minutes. Release pressure with a quick release. With sauté function, cook onions for about 5 minutes to reduce liquid.

Add stock and heat on medium until almost boiling. Add wine and salt. Reduce heat to low and simmer, uncovered, for 20 minutes to blend flavours.

Meanwhile place bread slices on an ungreased baking sheet. Broil on centre rack for about 3 minutes until golden. Turn slices. Sprinkle with cheese. Broil for about 3 minutes until cheese is melted and golden. Divide soup among 6 bowls. Top each with 2 cheese toasts. Serve immediately. Makes 6 servings.

*1 serving:* 620 Calories; 17 g Total Fat (7 g Mono, 2 g Poly, 7 g Sat); 25 mg Cholesterol; 90 g Carbohydrate (7 g Fibre, 11 g Sugar); 25 g Protein; 1500 mg Sodium

ᕬ For a baked version, broil the bread slices on one side only. Divide soup among 6 ovenproof bowls and place 2 bread slices in each bowl, toasted side down. Sprinkle about 3 tbsp. (45 mL) grated Gruyére (or mozzarella) cheese in each bowl. Broil for about 5 minutes until cheese is melted and golden. Serve immediately. Bowls will be very hot!

# Texas Chili

*A little like stew and a lot like chili—this all-in-one dish will make chili night exciting again! And the best part is you don't have to wait for hours as it cooks before you can enjoy it. Thanks to the multi-cooker, this chili has the complex flavour of a slow-cooked chili but is ready in less than an hour. Serve with garlic toast or whole-wheat buns and a fresh green salad to make a complete meal.*

| | | |
|---|---|---|
| Cooking oil | 2 tsp. | 10 mL |
| Boneless beef blade (or chuck) roast, trimmed of fat and cut into 1/2 inch (12 mm) pieces | 1 1/2 lbs. | 680 g |
| Salt | 1/4 tsp. | 1 mL |
| Pepper | 1/4 tsp. | 1 mL |
| Diced peeled potato | 2 cups | 500 mL |
| Chopped celery | 1 1/2 cups | 375 mL |
| Chopped onion | 1 1/2 cups | 375 mL |
| Prepared beef broth | 1 cup | 250 mL |
| Can of romano beans (19 oz., 540 mL), rinsed and drained | 1 | 1 |
| Can of diced tomatoes (14 oz., 398 mL), with juice | 1 | 1 |
| Bacon slices, cooked crisp and crumbled | 4 | 4 |
| Chili powder | 2 tbsp. | 30 mL |
| Brown sugar, packed | 1 tbsp. | 15 mL |
| Cocoa, sifted if lumpy | 1 tbsp. | 15 mL |
| Tomato paste (see Tip, page 41) | 1 tbsp. | 15 mL |
| Kernel corn | 1 cup | 250 mL |

With sauté function, heat cooking oil in inner pot on medium. Add beef. Sprinkle with salt and pepper. Cook for about 10 minutes, stirring occasionally, until browned. Remove from pot and set aside.

Add potato to inner pot and cook for 8 to 10 minutes. Remove from pot and set aside.

Add celery and onion to inner pot and cook, stirring, until onion is softened, about 3 to 5 minutes.

Stir in broth, scraping any brown bits from bottom of pan. Stir in next 7 ingredients. Turn off sauté function. Cover with lid and seal. Select pressure cooker function and cook on high pressure for 30 minutes. Allow pressure to release naturally. Stir in corn and potato and heat with sauté function on medium, stirring occasionally, until potato and corn are heated through. Makes about 9 cups (2.25 L).

*1 cup (250 mL): 420 Calories; 18 g Total Fat (10 g Mono, 2.5 g Poly, 8 g Sat); 75 mg Cholesterol; 32 g Carbohydrate (6 g Fibre, 6 g Sugar); 32 g Protein; 360 mg Sodium*

# Hearty Goulash Stew

*In this dish, traditional goulash is enhanced with smoked sweet paprika and harvest vegetables. There is quite a lot of prep work for this recipe, so if you want to save time and don't mind getting an extra frying pan dirty, you might want to brown the beef in a separate frying pan as the bacon is cooking in the inner pot. If you go this route, use the cooking oil to brown the beef, and cook the onion and garlic in the inner pot after you've cooked the bacon, using the reserved bacon fat.*

| | | |
|---|---|---|
| Cooking oil | 1 tbsp. | 15 mL |
| Chopped onion | 2 cups | 500 mL |
| Garlic cloves, minced (or 3/4 tsp., 4 mL, powder) | 3 | 3 |
| Bacon slices, diced | 8 | 8 |
| Stewing beef, trimmed of fat, cut into 3/4 inch (2 cm) pieces | 1 lb. | 454 g |
| Dry (or alcohol-free) red wine | 1/2 cup | 125 mL |
| Can of diced tomatoes (28 oz., 796 mL), with juice | 1 | 1 |
| Prepared beef broth | 2 cups | 500 mL |
| Chopped peeled potato | 1 1/2 cups | 375 mL |
| Chopped carrot | 1 cup | 250 mL |
| Chopped parsnip | 1 cup | 250 mL |
| Smoked (sweet) paprika | 1 tsp. | 5 mL |
| Salt | 1/2 tsp. | 2 mL |
| Pepper | 1/4 tsp. | 1 mL |

With sauté function, heat oil in inner pot on medium. Add onion and garlic and cook for about 10 minutes, stirring often, until onion starts to soften and brown. Transfer from inner pot to a large plate or bowl and set aside.

Add bacon to inner pot and cook on medium heat until crisp. Remove from pot with a slotted spoon. Drain and discard all but 2 tbsp. (30 mL) drippings.

Add beef to inner pot and cook on medium, stirring occasionally, until browned. Stir in bacon and onion mixture.

Stir in wine, scraping any brown bits from bottom of pot.

Add remaining 8 ingredients. Turn off sauté function. Cover with lid and seal. Select pressure cooker function. Cook on high pressure for 30 minutes. Allow pressure to release naturally. Makes about 10 cups (2.5 L).

*1 cup (250 mL): 300 Calories; 11 g Total Fat (4.5 g Mono, 1 g Poly, 4 g Sat); 45 mg Cholesterol; 26 g Carbohydrate (4 g Fibre, 10 g Sugar); 20 g Protein; 690 mg Sodium*

# Italian Pot Roast

*Usually when one thinks "pot roast," one pictures a long cooking time in the oven or slow cooker, but with the pressure cooking function on your multi-cooker, you can cut the cooking time down to just over an hour. The end result is tender, delicious meat with plenty of tasty sauce to serve over pasta, potatoes or polenta.*

| | | |
|---|---|---|
| Boneless beef blade (or chuck) roast | 3 lbs. | 1.4 kg |
| Salt | 1/2 tsp. | 2 mL |
| Pepper | 1/4 tsp. | 1 mL |
| Olive oil | 2 tsp. | 10 mL |
| Bacon slices, chopped | 2 | 2 |
| Chopped onion | 1 1/2 cups | 375 mL |
| Chopped celery | 1 cup | 250 mL |
| Dried oregano | 1 tsp. | 5 mL |
| Garlic cloves, minced (or 1/2 tsp., 2 mL, powder) | 2 | 2 |
| Prepared beef broth | 2 cups | 500 mL |
| Can of diced tomatoes (28 oz., 796 mL), drained | 1 | 1 |
| Dry (or alcohol-free) red wine | 1/2 cup | 125 mL |
| Bay leaves | 2 | 2 |
| All-purpose flour | 1/4 cup | 60 mL |
| Water | 1/2 cup | 125 mL |

Sprinkle roast with salt and pepper. With sauté function heat olive oil in inner pot on medium. Add roast. Cook for about 10 minutes, turning occasionally, until browned on all sides. Transfer to a large plate.

Add bacon to inner pot. Cook for about 3 minutes, stirring often, until almost crisp. Add next 4 ingredients. Cook for about 8 minutes, stirring often, until onion starts to soften.

Slowly add broth, stirring constantly and scraping any brown bits from bottom of pot, until smooth. Stir in next 3 ingredients. Turn off sauté function. Add roast. Cover with lid and seal. Select pressure cooker function and cook on high pressure for 1 hour. Allow pressure to release naturally. Remove roast to a cutting board. Cover with foil and let stand for 10 minutes. Slice roast.

Remove and discard bay leaves from sauce. Skim and discard fat. Stir flour into water until smooth. Add to sauce. With sauté function, heat sauce on low, stirring, until thickened. Serve with roast. Makes 10 servings.

*1 cup (250 mL): 420 Calories; 28 g Total Fat (12 g Mono, 1.5 g Poly, 11 g Sat); 105 mg Cholesterol; 10 g Carbohydrate (2 g Fibre, 4 g Sugar); 28 g Protein; 710 mg Sodium*

# Lazy Cabbage Roll Casserole

*This delicious casserole has all the classic cabbage roll flavours without the fussy rolling.*

| | | |
|---|---|---|
| Bacon slices, chopped | 4 | 4 |
| Chopped onion | 2 cups | 500 mL |
| Lean ground beef | 1 lb. | 454 g |
| Garlic cloves, minced | 2 | 2 |
| (or 1/2 tsp., 2 mL, powder) | | |
| Celery seed | 1/2 tsp. | 2 mL |
| Pepper | 1/2 tsp. | 2 mL |
| Coarsely chopped cabbage | 3 cups | 750 mL |
| Long-grain brown rice | 1 1/2 cups | 375 mL |
| Coarsely chopped cabbage | 3 cups | 750 mL |
| Can of diced tomatoes (28 oz., 796 mL), with juice | 1 | 1 |
| Prepared vegetable broth | 2 cups | 500 mL |
| Hot pepper sauce | 1/2 tsp. | 2 mL |

With sauté function, sauté bacon in inner pot on medium heat until crisp. Transfer with a slotted spoon to a plate lined with paper towel to drain. Drain and discard all but 1 tsp. (5 mL) drippings.

Add next 5 ingredients. Scramble-fry for about 10 minutes until beef is no longer pink. Turn off sauté function. Remove beef mixture from pot and drain.

Layer first amount of cabbage in inner pot and spread beef mixture over top. Scatter rice and bacon over beef mixture and layer second amount of cabbage over bacon.

Combine remaining 3 ingredients in a medium bowl. Pour over top. Do not stir. Cover with lid and seal. Select the pressure cooker function and cook on high pressure for 5 minutes. Allow pressure to release naturally for 10 minutes and then do a quick release of the remaining pressure. Makes about 12 cups (3 L).

*1 cup (250 mL):* 270 Calories; 10 g Total Fat (4.5 g Mono, 1 g Poly, 3.5 g Sat); 35 mg Cholesterol; 28 g Carbohydrate (30 g Fibre, 5 g Sugar); 16 g Protein; 530 mg Sodium

# Beef and Herb Ragout

*This rich, flavourful pasta sauce looks more like a stew than a sauce. Serve it over your favourite long pasta, with a green salad and garlic bread on the side for a filling meal. To save on prep time, you could use stewing beef in place of the blade steak and brown the meat on the stovetop as the onions and celery sauté in the inner pot.*

| | | |
|---|---|---|
| Cooking oil | 1 tsp. | 5 mL |
| Chopped celery | 1 cup | 250 mL |
| Chopped onion | 1 cup | 250 mL |
| | | |
| Cooking oil | 2 tsp. | 10 mL |
| Boneless beef blade steak, trimmed of fat, cut into 1 inch (2.5 cm) cubes | 1 1/2 lbs. | 680 g |
| | | |
| Dry (or alcohol-free) white wine | 1/2 cup | 125 mL |
| | | |
| Can of crushed tomatoes (14 oz., 398 mL) | 1 | 1 |
| Chopped carrot | 1 cup | 250 mL |
| Chopped purple-topped turnip | 1 cup | 250 mL |
| Chopped fresh rosemary (or 3/4 tsp., 4 mL, dried, crushed) | 1 tbsp. | 15 mL |
| Bay leaf | 1 | 1 |
| Garlic clove, minced (or 1/4 tsp., 1 mL, powder) | 1 | 1 |
| | | |
| Salt | 1/2 tsp. | 2 mL |
| Pepper | 1/2 tsp. | 2 mL |
| Grated Parmesan cheese | 1/4 cup | 60 mL |
| Half-and-half cream | 3 tbsp. | 45 mL |
| Chopped fresh parsley (or 3/4 tsp., 4 mL, flakes) | 1 tbsp. | 15 mL |
| Chopped fresh rosemary | 1 tsp. | 5 mL |
| Grated orange zest | 1/4 tsp. | 1 mL |

With sauté function, heat first amount of cooking oil in inner pot on medium. Add celery and onion. Cook for about 8 minutes, stirring often, until onion is softened. Remove from pot and set aside.

Heat second amount of cooking oil on medium. Add beef and cook, in 2 batches, for about 5 minutes, stirring occasionally, until browned.

Add celery mixture and wine. Stir, scraping any brown bits from bottom of pot, until boiling.

Stir in beef and next 8 ingredients. Turn off sauté function. Cover with lid and seal. Select the pressure cooker function and cook on high pressure for 30 minutes. Do a quick release of the pressure. Remove and discard bay leaf.

Stir in remaining 5 ingredients. Makes about 5 cups (1.25 L).

*1 cup (250 mL):* 470 Calories; 29 g Total Fat (13 g Mono, 2 g Poly, 11 g Sat); 85 mg Cholesterol; 17 g Carbohydrate (4 g Fibre, 8 g Sugar); 28 g Protein; 640 mg Sodium

# Curry Coconut Ribs

*Once you have tried cooking ribs in the pressure cooker, you'll never want to prepare them any other way. They cook in much less time than they do in the oven, and the end result is tender, fall-off-the-bone meat.*

| | | |
|---|---|---|
| Cooking oil | 1/2 tsp. | 2 mL |
| Red curry paste | 1 tbsp. | 15 mL |
| Can of coconut milk (14 oz., 398 mL) | 1 | 1 |
| Brown sugar, packed | 3 tbsp. | 45 mL |
| Soy sauce | 3 tbsp. | 45 mL |
| Lime juice | 2 tbsp. | 30 mL |
| Garlic cloves, sliced | 5 | 5 |
| Ginger root slices (1/4 inch, 6 mm, thick) | 4 | 4 |
| Seasoned salt | 1 tbsp. | 15 mL |
| Racks of pork side ribs (about 1 1/2 lbs., 680 g, each) trimmed of fat and cut into 2-bone portions | 2 | 2 |

With sauté function, heat cooking oil in inner pot on medium. Add curry paste and cook, stirring, for about 1 minute until fragrant.

Add next 4 ingredients. Simmer for 10 minutes to blend flavours.

Stir next 3 ingredients into inner pot and add ribs. Cover with lid and seal. Select pressure cooker function and cook on high pressure for 25 minutes. Allow pressure to release naturally. Makes about 12 portions.

*1 portion:* *440 Calories; 32 g Total Fat (11 g Mono, 2.5 g Poly, 15 g Sat); 120 mg Cholesterol; 6 g Carbohydrate (0 g Fibre, 4 g Sugar); 32 g Protein; 1010 mg Sodium*

# Pork Jambalaya

*Bring the flavours of Louisiana to your kitchen with our take on this Cajun classic.*

| | | |
|---|---|---|
| **Hot sausage links (such as Chorizo or hot Italian), cut into 1/2 inch (12 mm) pieces** | 1 lb. | 454 g |
| **Lean pork, cut into bite size pieces** | 1 1/2 lbs. | 680 g |
| **Long grain white rice, uncooked** | 1 1/2 cups | 375 mL |
| **Chopped onion** | 1 cup | 250 mL |
| **Chopped celery** | 1/3 cup | 75 mL |
| **Low sodium beef broth** | 3 cups | 750 mL |
| **Salsa** | 1/2 cup | 125 mL |
| **Cayenne pepper** | 1/2 tsp. | 2 mL |
| **Garlic powder** | 1/4 tsp. | 1 mL |
| **Salt** | 1/2 tsp. | 2 mL |
| **Pepper** | 1/4 tsp. | 1 mL |

With sauté function, cook sausage pieces in inner pot on high until browned. Add pork and cook, stirring, for 1 to 2 minutes until firm. Turn off sauté function. Drain fat from inner pot.

Pour rice evenly over meat. Scatter onion and celery over rice.

Mix remaining 6 ingredients in a medium bowl. Pour over celery and onion. Cover with lid and seal. Select pressure cooker function and cook on high pressure for 15 minutes. Allow pressure to drop naturally. Makes 9 servings.

*1 serving: 390 Calories; 22 g Total Fat (10 g Mono, 1 g Poly, 8 g Sat); 105 mg Cholesterol; 12 g Carbohydrate (1 g Fibre, 2 g Sugar); 34 g Protein; 950 mg Sodium*

# Chili Lime Pork Ragout

*This ragout is loaded with nutritious spinach and has plenty of sweet sauce flavoured with lime and cilantro—great for serving over couscous, rice or barley. If you are planning on making this dish as a weekday meal, you might want to precut your meat and sweet potatoes.*

| | | |
|---|---|---|
| Canola oil | 1 tbsp. | 15 mL |
| Boneless pork shoulder blade steaks, trimmed of fat, cut into 1 inch (2.5 cm) cubes | 2 lbs. | 900 g |
| Chopped onion | 1 1/2 cups | 375 mL |
| Chili powder | 2 tsp. | 10 mL |
| Garlic powder | 1/2 tsp. | 2 mL |
| Salt | 1/2 tsp. | 2 mL |
| Cayenne pepper | 1/4 tsp. | 1 mL |
| Prepared chicken broth | 1/2 cup | 125 mL |
| Water | 1/2 cup | 125 mL |
| Cubed peeled orange-fleshed sweet potato | 5 cups | 1.25 L |
| Chopped fresh spinach leaves, lightly packed | 2 cups | 500 mL |
| Chopped fresh cilantro (or parsley) | 1 tbsp. | 15 mL |
| Lime juice | 1 tbsp. | 15 mL |
| Liquid honey | 2 tsp. | 10 mL |
| Grated lime zest | 1 tsp. | 5 mL |

With sauté function, heat canola oil on medium. Cook pork, in 2 batches, for about 5 minutes, stirring occasionally, until browned. Transfer to a large plate of bowl and set aside.

Add onion to inner pot. Cook for about 5 minutes, stirring often, until onion starts to soften. Add next 4 ingredients. Heat, stirring, for 1 minute. Stir in broth and water, scraping any brown bits from bottom of pot. Turn off sauté function.

Add pork and sweet potato. Cover with lid and seal. Select pressure cooker function and cook on high pressure for 25 minutes. Allow pressure to release naturally.

Stir in remaining 5 ingredients. Makes about 7 1/2 cups (1.9 L).

*1 cup (250 mL): 390 Calories; 17 g Total Fat (8 g Mono, 2 g Poly, 6 g Sat); 100 mg Cholesterol; 27 g Carbohydrate (4 g Fibre, 7 g Sugar); 31 g Protein; 300 mg Sodium*

# "Baked" Ham

*Ham is another perfect dish to cook in the multi-cooker. Not only do you free up space in your oven for sides (or dessert!), but with the pressure cooker function, your ham will perfectly cooked in less time than it would take in the oven.*

| | | |
|---|---|---|
| Water | 1 cup | 250 mL |
| Smoked ham, bone in | 3 lbs. | 1.4 kg |
| (not frozen, see Note) | | |
| Brown sugar, packed | 1/2 cup | 125 mL |
| Frozen concentrated orange juice, thawed | 2 tbsp. | 30 mL |
| Dijon mustard (with whole seeds) | 1 tbsp. | 15 mL |
| Prepared horseradish | 2 tsp. | 10 mL |
| Lemon juice | 3 tbsp. | 45 mL |
| Cornstarch | 2 tbsp. | 30 mL |

Add water to inner pot. Place ham on a trivet and lower into pot.

Combine next 4 ingredients in a small dish. Pour over ham. Cover with lid and seal. Select pressure cooker function and cook on high pressure for 30 minutes. Allow pressure to release naturally. Transfer ham to a cutting board and cut into thin slices. Arrange on a serving platter and cover to keep warm.

Stir lemon juice into cornstarch in a small cup and slowly add to inner pot. With sauté function, heat mixture on medium, stirring constantly, until boiling and thickened. Drizzle over ham slices. Makes 8 servings.

*1 serving: 290 Calories; 10 g Total Fat (4.5 g Mono, 1 g Poly, 3 g Sat); 95 mg Cholesterol; 19 g Carbohydrate (0 g Fibre, 16 g Sugar); 29 g Protein; 2000 mg Sodium*

**Note**: A ham that's been frozen adds too much moisture, which could affect the quality of this dish.

# Larry's 9-Bean Soup

*A warm thank you to Larry Palmeter for sharing this recipe with us! You can use a commercially prepared 9-bean soup mix or make your own. We've soaked the beans overnight, but if you forget to presoak your beans, don't fret. The multi-cooker is great for cooking un-soaked beans, too, though they tend to burst more often than presoaked ones do. If you are using un-soaked beans, increase the cooking time by about half.*

| | | |
|---|---|---|
| 9-bean soup mix, soaked overnight, rinsed and drained | 1 1/2 cups | 375 mL |
| Leftover meaty ham bone | 1 | 1 |
| Water, to cover | | |
| Chopped ham | 1 cup | 250 mL |
| Medium onion, chopped | 1 | 1 |
| Can of diced tomatoes (14 oz., 398 mL), with juice | 1 | 1 |
| Carrots, chopped | 3 | 3 |
| Celery ribs, chopped | 2 | 2 |
| Chili powder | 1 tsp. | 5 mL |
| Garlic powder | 1 tsp. | 5 mL |
| Seasoning salt | 1 tsp. | 5 mL |
| Pepper | 1/4 tsp. | 2 mL |

Add bean mix and ham bone to inner pot and add enough water to cover. Cover with lid and seal. Select pressure cooker function and cook for 30 minutes on high pressure. Allow pressure to release naturally. Remove all meat from bone and discard bone. Chop meat and return to inner pot.

Add next 9 ingredients. Cover with lid and seal. Select pressure cooker function and cook for 20 minutes. The multi-cooker will come back up to pressure quickly because the contents are hot. Allow pressure to release naturally. Makes 8 servings.

*1 serving:* *380 Calories; 1 g Total Fat (0 g Mono, 0 g Poly, 0 g Sat); 10 mg Cholesterol; 33 g Carbohydrate (10 g Fibre, 3 g Sugar); 13 g Protein; 580 mg Sodium*

# Lamb Curry

*This delicious curry is based on a variation from southern India. Serve it over couscous, rice or noodles.*

| | | |
|---|---|---|
| Boneless lamb, trimmed of fat, cubed | 3 lbs. | 1.4 kg |
| Large onion, chopped | 1 | 1 |
| Grated carrot | 1/2 cup | 125 mL |
| Beef broth | 1 cup | 250 mL |
| Curry powder | 2 tsp. | 10 mL |
| Ground ginger | 1/8 tsp. | 0.5 mL |
| Ground cumin | 1/8 tsp. | 0.5 mL |
| Pepper | 1/4 tsp. | 1 mL |
| Medium coconut | 1/4 cup | 60 mL |
| Cornstarch | 2 tbsp. | 30 mL |
| Water | 2 tbsp. | 30 mL |
| Mango chutney | 1/2 cup | 125 mL |

Combine lamb, onion and carrot in inner pot of multi-cooker.

Stir next 6 ingredients in a small bowl and add to lamb mixture. Cover with lid and seal. Select pressure cooker function and cook on high pressure for 15 minutes. Allow pressure to release naturally.

Mix cornstarch and water in a small cup and stir into curry. With sauté function, simmer on low until thickened. Stir in chutney. Makes 10 servings.

*1 serving: 310 Calories; 22 g Total Fat (9 g Mono, 2 g Poly, 10 g Sat); 80 mg Cholesterol; 4 g Carbohydrate (1 g Fibre, 10 g Sugar); 21 g Protein; 140 mg Sodium*

# The Sauté Function

If you are new to the multi-cooker, you might wonder why you would ever use such a large machine to sauté your food. After all, you are not likely to haul out your multi-cooker to pan-fry a burger or sauté some mushrooms to go along with your grilled steak. Your frying pan and the burner on your stove top can do the job easier and possibly with less clean up, if your frying pan has a non-stick coating. So taken by itself, the sauté function might not seem all that useful.

However, the sauté function is what makes the multi-cooker a one-pot cooking experience. This function allows you to brown meat or vegetables in the inner pot before choosing the pressure cooker or slow cooker function. Traditional pressure cookers and slow cookers would have you prepare this first step in a separate frying pan before adding the sautéed food to the cooker of choice. With the multi-cooker's humble sauté function, you'll have no extra pans to wash.

The sauté function also allows you to cook off extra liquid or reduce sauces after the pressure cooker or slow cooker cycle has finished. Is your beef ragout a little too watery? No worries. Just switch on the sauté function, and cook it a little longer until it thickens up to your liking.

The sauté function is also useful for finishing off a dish that might be a little undercooked coming out of the pressure cooker. If you are not sure how long to cook your dish under pressure, it is always best to err on the side of caution and cook it for a little less time. You can't uncook food that has been cooked for too long, but you can use the sauté function to finish off a dish that would benefit from a little bit more cooking time.

Most multi-cooker sauté functions allow you to choose between low, medium and high heat. Medium heat is the most commonly used setting and will be the one you use to fulfill most of your sautéing needs; high is perfect for quickly searing a cut of meat; and low is best used for reducing sauces or simmering soups and the like. If your particular multi-cooker does not have the ability to switch between high, medium and low heat, simply turn the cooker off from time to time to keep the heat at the level you need for your recipe.

When using the sauté function, make sure the lid of the multi-cooker is off. If the lid is on, the cooker might start to build up pressure. If you really need to cover your food as it is sautéing or simmering, use a lid from one of your other cooking pots or pans that will fit the multi-cooker, and set it so that it does not cover the entire opening of the inner pot, and the steam has some room to escape.

# Spice Chicken

*Cook a whole chicken in the multi-cooker? You bet! A good rule of thumb is to cook the chicken for 6 minutes per pound. The end result is the most tender, moist chicken you will ever experience. If you prefer crispy skin, stick the chicken under the broiler for a few minutes to brown it, but make sure to watch it carefully so it doesn't burn.*

| | | |
|---|---|---|
| Garlic cloves, minced | 2 | 2 |
| Balsamic vinegar | 1/2 tbsp. | 7 mL |
| Butter (or hard margarine), softened | 1/2 tbsp. | 7 mL |
| Dried oregano | 1/2 tbsp. | 7 mL |
| Frozen concentrated orange juice, thawed | 1/2 tbsp. | 7 mL |
| Ground cumin | 1/2 tbsp. | 7 mL |
| Salt | 1/2 tsp. | 2 mL |
| Pepper | 1 tsp. | 2 mL |
| Water | 1 cup | 250 mL |
| Whole chicken | 3 lbs. | 1.4 kg |

Stir first 8 ingredients in a small bowl until mixture forms a smooth paste.

Add water and trivet to inner pot of multi-cooker. Carefully loosen chicken skin on breast and thighs but do not remove. Stuff paste between meat and skin, spreading mixture as evenly as possible. Tie wings with butcher string close to body. Tie legs to tail and place on trivet. Cover with lid and seal. Select pressure cooker function and cook on high pressure for 18 minutes. Let pressure release naturally for 20 minutes, then do a quick release of any remaining pressure. Transfer chicken to a cutting board. Remove and discard butcher string. Cover chicken with foil and let stand for 10 minutes before carving. Makes 4 servings.

*1 serving: 460 Calories; 15 g Total Fat (4 g Mono, 3 g Poly, 5 g Sat); 255 mg Cholesterol; 3 g Carbohydrate (0 g Fibre, 0 g Sugar); 75 g Protein; 890 mg Sodium*

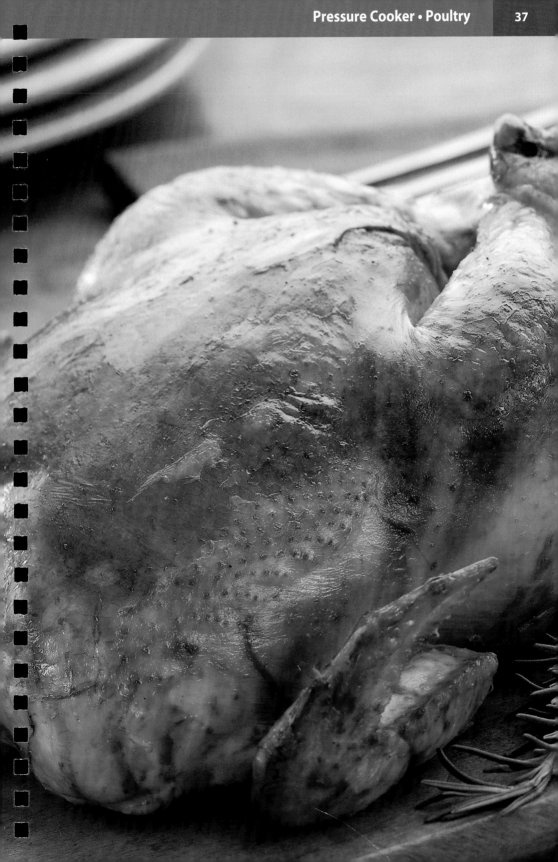

# Chicken Vegetable Gumbo

*Although you should not add thickeners to your multi-cooker until after the pressure cooking cycle is complete, the flour in this recipe acts as a flavouring agent rather than a thickener and gives the gumbo a touch of nuttiness.*

| | | |
|---|---|---|
| Canola oil | 3 tbsp. | 45 mL |
| All-purpose flour | 3 tbsp. | 45 mL |
| Chopped celery | 1 1/2 cups | 375 mL |
| Chopped green pepper | 1 1/2 cups | 375 mL |
| Chopped onion | 1 1/2 cups | 375 mL |
| Dried oregano | 1 tsp. | 5 mL |
| Dried thyme | 1 tsp. | 5 mL |
| Dry mustard | 1/2 tsp. | 2 mL |
| Garlic powder | 1/2 tsp. | 2 mL |
| Pepper | 1/4 tsp. | 1 mL |
| Low-sodium prepared chicken broth | 3 cups | 750 mL |
| Tomato juice | 1 cup | 250 mL |
| Bay leaves | 2 | 2 |
| Boneless, skinless chicken thighs, trimmed of fat, cut into 1 inch (2.5 cm) pieces | 1 lb. | 454 g |
| Sliced fresh (or frozen, thawed) okra (1/2 inch, 12 mm, pieces) | 2 cups | 500 mL |
| Sliced kielbasa (or other spiced cooked lean sausage), 1/4 inch (6 mm) pieces | 1 cup | 250 mL |
| Cooked long-grain brown rice (about 2/3 cup, 150 mL, uncooked) | 2 cups | 500 mL |
| Chopped seeded tomato | 1 cup | 250 mL |
| Hot pepper sauce | 1 tbsp. | 15 mL |

With sauté function, heat canola oil in inner pot on medium. Add flour and cook, stirring, for about 9 minutes until browned.

Add next 11 ingredients. Heat, stirring, until boiling and thickened. Turn off sauté function.

Add next 3 ingredients. Cover with lid and seal. Select pressure cooker function and cook on high pressure for 20 minutes. Allow pressure to release naturally. Skim and discard fat. Remove and discard bay leaves.

Stir in remaining 3 ingredients. With sauté function, cook on medium, stirring occasionally, for about 15 minutes until heated through. Makes about 11 1/2 cups (2.9 L).

*1 cup (250 mL):* 230 Calories; 11 g Total Fat (4.5 g Mono, 3.5 g Poly, 2.5 g Sat); 45 mg Cholesterol; 18 g Carbohydrate (3 g Fibre, 4 g Sugar); 16 g Protein; 340 mg Sodium

# Coq au Vin Blanc

*This white wine version of a French favourite offers a more subtle flavour than the traditional red—but the taste experience is just as exquisite! Pairs well with mashed potatoes.*

| | | |
|---|---|---|
| Bacon slices, cut into 1 inch (2.5 cm) pieces | 6 | 6 |
| Cooking oil | 1 tsp. | 5 mL |
| Bone-in chicken thighs | 8 | 8 |
| (about 5 oz., 140 g, each) | | |
| Salt | 1/2 tsp. | 2 mL |
| Pepper | 1/2 tsp. | 2 mL |
| Halved fresh brown (or white) mushrooms | 3 cups | 750 mL |
| Garlic clove, minced | 1 | 1 |
| (or 1/4 tsp., 1 mL, powder) | | |
| Dry (or alcohol-free) white wine | 1/2 cup | 125 mL |
| Prepared chicken broth | 1 cup | 250 mL |
| Brandy | 1/4 cup | 60 mL |
| Tomato paste (see Tip, page 41) | 2 tbsp. | 30 mL |
| Pearl onions | 5 oz. | 140 g |
| Bay leaf | 1 | 1 |
| Dried thyme | 1/2 tsp. | 2 mL |
| All-purpose flour | 2 tbsp. | 30 mL |
| Water | 1/4 cup | 60 mL |

With sauté function, cook bacon in inner pot on medium until crisp. Transfer with a slotted spoon to a plate lined with paper towel. Reserve 2 tbsp. (30 mL) drippings in a small cup. Discard remaining drippings.

Heat cooking oil in inner pot. Sprinkle both sides of chicken with salt and pepper. Add to pot and cook for about 5 minutes per side, until browned. Transfer to a plate and cover to keep warm.

Heat reserved drippings in inner pot. Add mushrooms and garlic and cook for about 5 minutes, stirring occasionally, until mushrooms are golden.

Slowly add next 4 ingredients, stirring constantly until smooth.

Stir in next 3 ingredients, bacon and chicken. Turn off sauté function. Cover with lid and seal. Select pressure cooker function and cook at high pressure for 15 minutes. Allow pressure to release naturally for 10 minutes, then do a quick release of remaining pressure. Using a slotted spoon, transfer chicken to a serving dish.

Combine flour and water in a small cup. Add to sauce in pot. With sauté function, simmer until sauce is thickened. Remove and discard bay leaf. Makes 4 servings.

*1 serving: 750 Calories; 36 g Total Fat (15 g Mono, 8 g Poly, 10 g Sat); 175 mg Cholesterol; 32 g Carbohydrate (5 g Fibre, 7 g Sugar); 47 g Protein; 1030 mg Sodium*

**Tip:** Try freezing tomato paste for 30 minutes before opening both ends and pushing the tube out. You'll be able to slice off what you need and wrap the rest for later.

# Mango Chipotle Chicken

*With the pressure cooker function on your multi-cooker, this recipe is easy to prepare but elegant enough to serve to company. The fruity sauce tastes great over rice.*

| | | |
|---|---|---|
| Cooking oil | 2 tbsp. | 30 mL |
| Boneless, skinless chicken thighs, halved | 3 lbs. | 1.4 kg |
| Chili powder | 2 tbsp. | 30 mL |
| Granulated sugar | 1 tsp. | 5 mL |
| Salt | 1 tsp. | 5 mL |
| Pepper | 1/4 tsp. | 1 mL |
| Chopped onion | 2 cups | 500 mL |
| Chopped yellow pepper | 1 1/2 cups | 375 mL |
| Chopped red pepper | 1 1/2 cups | 375 mL |
| Guava juice (or nectar) | 1 cup | 250 mL |
| Finely chopped chipotle peppers in adobo sauce (see Tip, below) | 1 tbsp. | 15 mL |
| Tomato paste (see Tip, page 41) | 1 tbsp. | 15 mL |
| Chopped fresh (or frozen, thawed and drained) mango | 2 cups | 500 mL |
| Chopped fresh cilantro | 1/4 cup | 60 mL |
| Lime juice | 1 tbsp. | 15 mL |

With sauté function, heat 2 tsp. (10 mL) cooking oil in inner pot on high. Add a third of chicken. Cook for about 1 minute per side until browned. Transfer to a large plate. Repeat with remaining chicken and oil. Turn off sauté function. Return all chicken to inner pot. Add next 4 ingredients and stir well. Add next 3 ingredients in order given.

Combine next 3 ingredients in a separate small bowl. Pour over top. Cover with lid and seal. Select pressure cooker function and cook on high pressure for 20 minutes. Allow pressure to release naturally.

Stir in remaining 3 ingredients. Makes about 10 cups (2.5 mL).

*1 cup (250 mL): 280 Calories; 10 g Total Fat (1.5 g Mono, 1 g Poly, 0 g Sat); 100 mg Cholesterol; 20 g Carbohydrate (4 g Fibre, 11 g Sugar); 28 g Protein; 290 mg Sodium*

**Tip:** Chipotle chili peppers in adobo sauce are smoked jalapeño peppers that are canned in a smoky red sauce. Adobo sauce is not as spicy as the chipotle pepper, but it still packs some heat. Be sure to wash your hands after handling. Store leftover chipotle chili peppers with sauce in airtight container in refrigerator for up to 1 year.

# Pulled Tex Turkey

*This twist on the traditional pulled pork uses turkey instead of pork and replaces the usual long, drawn-out slow-cooking method with a quick stint in the pressure cooker. All of the flavour without the long wait. What could be better?*

| | | |
|---|---|---|
| Sliced onion | 1 1/2 cups | 375 mL |
| Barbecue sauce | 1 cup | 250 mL |
| Can of tomato sauce (7 1/2 oz., 213 mL) | 1 | 1 |
| Can of diced green chilies (4 oz., 113 g) | 1 | 1 |
| Chili powder | 1 tbsp. | 15 mL |
| Dried oregano | 1 tsp. | 5 mL |
| Ground cumin | 1/2 tsp. | 2 mL |
| Ground cinnamon | 1/4 tsp. | 1 mL |
| Boneless, skinless turkey thighs | 1 3/4 lbs. | 790 g |
| Kaiser rolls, split | 6 | 6 |

Combine first 8 ingredients in inner pot. Add turkey and spoon barbecue sauce mixture over top so turkey is fully covered. Cover with lid and seal. Select pressure cooker function and cook on high pressure for 20 minutes. Allow pressure to release naturally. Remove turkey to a cutting board using tongs. Shred turkey using 2 forks. Return to sauce mixture and stir.

Serve turkey mixture in rolls. Makes 6 sandwiches.

*1 sandwich: 400 Calories; 6 g Total Fat (1.5 g Mono, 2 g Poly, 1 g Sat); 80 mg Cholesterol; 46 g Carbohydrate (4 g Fibre, 9 g Sugar); 39 g Protein; 1010 mg Sodium*

# Chicken Cacciatore

*Serve this classic Italian dish with penne or your favorite pasta and a fresh green salad.*

| | | |
|---|---|---|
| Cooking oil | 1 tbsp. | 15 mL |
| Boneless, skinless chicken breast halves (about 1 lb., 454 g) | 4 | 4 |
| Medium onion, sliced | 1 | 1 |
| Garlic cloves, minced | 2 | 2 |
| Sliced fresh mushrooms | 1 cup | 250 mL |
| Small green pepper, chopped (optional) | 1 | 1 |
| Can of diced tomatoes (14 oz., 398 mL), with juice | 1 | 1 |
| Apple juice | 1/2 cup | 125 mL |
| Dried whole oregano | 1 tsp. | 2 mL |
| Dried sweet basil | 1 tsp. | 1 mL |
| Granulated sugar | 1/2 tsp. | 2 mL |
| Salt | 1/2 tsp. | 2 mL |
| Pepper | 1/4 tsp. | 1 mL |
| Ground rosemary | 1/2 tsp. | 0.5 mL |

Using sauté function, warm oil in inner pot over medium heat. Add chicken and cook until browned. Turn off sauté function.

Add onion, garlic, mushrooms and green pepper.

Stir remaining 8 ingredients together in a medium bowl. Pour over chicken. Cover and seal lid. Select pressure cooker function and cook on high pressure for 10 minutes. Let pressure release naturally. Makes 4 servings.

*1 serving:* 540 Calories; 26 g Total Fat (12 g Mono, 6 g Poly, 7 g Sat); 200 mg Cholesterol; 17 g Carbohydrate (3 g Fibre, 10 g Sugar); 58 g Protein; 750 mg Sodium

# "Boiled" Eggs in the Multi-cooker

Cooking eggs in the multi-cooker might at first glance seem like a waste of effort when you can simply boil them in a pot on the stove. And it is true that, when you factor in the time it takes for the machine to build and then release pressure, it might not be much quicker to cook your eggs in the multi-cooker. In fact, depending on how many eggs you are cooking and how much water you have in the pot, the trusted pot-on-stove method might be slightly quicker. So why bother cooking eggs in the multi-cooker, you ask?

The real benefit will be obvious as soon as the time comes to peel the eggs. Once you have peeled an egg that was cooked in the multi-cooker, you'll leave your pot in the cupboard, where it belongs. Eggs from a multi-cooker peel like dream! No more standing at the sink cursing under your breath as little fragments of shell break off at a time, taking chunks of egg white with them. With multi-cooker eggs, the shell comes off easily and in large sections, leaving the egg beneath fully intact.

We'll leave it up to you to decide whether the eggs taste better, too…

# "Hard-boiled" Eggs

**6 eggs**
**1 cup water**

To cook eggs in your multi-cooker, place the trivet in the inner pot and add the water. Place the eggs on the trivet. Cover with the lid and seal. Select the pressure cooker function and cook on high pressure for 5 minutes. Allow the pressure to release naturally for 5 minutes, and then release any remaining pressure with a quick release.

For a less firm yolk, reduce the cooking time to 4 minutes. For a soft yolk, reduce the time to 3 minutes, and do a quick release of the pressure. The cooking time does not change no matter how many eggs you cook at one time.

To save time and stress on our busy weekday mornings, we like to cook enough eggs on the weekend to last the entire work/school week. The cooked eggs will last in the fridge for up to a week as long as they are not peeled, and they peel as easily on day 6 as they do on the day they were first cooked.

# Seafood Chowder

*As a rule, fish and seafood don't tend to fare well when cooked with high pressure, but this delicious chowder is an exception to the rule. A must-try.*

| | | |
|---|---|---|
| Bacon slices, diced | 3 | 3 |
| Medium onion, chopped | 1 | 1 |
| Grated potato | 2 cups | 500 mL |
| Medium carrot, grated | 1 | 1 |
| Finely chopped celery | 1/4 cup | 60 mL |
| Chicken broth | 3 1/2 cups | 875 mL |
| Cod fillet (10 oz., 284 mL), cubed | 1 | 1 |
| All-purpose flour | 1/4 cup | 60 mL |
| Salt | 1 tsp. | 5 mL |
| Pepper | 1/8 tsp. | 0.5 mL |
| Skim evaporated milk | 1 cup | 250 mL |
| Chopped cooked shrimp | 1 cup | 250 mL |

With sauté function, cook bacon and onion on medium until golden. Turn off sauté function.

Add next 5 ingredients. Cover with lid and seal. Select pressure cooker function and cook on high pressure for 3 minutes. Allow pressure to release naturally.

With sauté function, heat chowder until gently boiling. Combine flour, salt and pepper in small bowl. Gradually whisk in milk until mixture is smooth. Add to boiling soup and cook, stirring constantly, until thickened.

Add shrimp and cook until shrimp are heated through. Makes 8 3/4 cups (2.2 L).

*1 cup (250 mL): 170 Calories; 6 g Total Fat (2 g Mono, .5 g Poly, 2 g Sat); 55 mg Cholesterol; 16 g Carbohydrate (1 g Fibre, 1 g Sugar); 15 g Protein; 790 mg Sodium*

# Acorn Apple Soup

*This sweet 'n' spicy blend of autumn flavours is simply sensational. If you don't want to brown the squash seeds in the inner pot before you prepare the soup, you can always use the oven method: spread the seeds evenly in an ungreased shallow pan and bake in a 300°F (150°C) oven for about 20 minutes, stirring or shaking often, until they are crisp and golden.*

| | | |
|---|---|---|
| Cooking oil | 1 tsp. | 5 mL |
| Salt | 1/8 tsp. | 0.5 mL |
| Reserved acorn squash seeds, rinsed and dried | 1/2 cup | 125 mL |
| Acorn squash, chopped (about 8 cups, 2 L), reserving 1/2 cup (125 mL) seeds | 2 1/2 lbs. | 1.1 kg |
| Tart medium cooking apples (such as Granny Smith), peeled and cores removed, chopped | 4 | 4 |
| Prepared chicken (or vegetable) broth | 3 cups | 750 mL |
| Chopped peeled potato | 1 cup | 250 mL |
| Applesauce | 1/2 cup | 125 mL |
| Chopped onion | 1/2 cup | 125 mL |
| Bay leaves | 2 | 2 |
| Finely grated, peeled ginger root | 1 tbsp. | 15 mL |
| Ground nutmeg | 1/4 tsp. | 1 mL |

With sauté function, heat cooking oil and salt in inner pot on medium. Add squash seeds and toss until coated. Cook seeds until crisp and golden, about 10 minutes. Turn off sauté function. Remove seeds from pot and set aside.

Combine remaining 9 ingredients in inner pot. Cover with lid and seal. Select pressure cooker function and cook on high pressure for 8 minutes. Allow pressure to decrease naturally. Remove and discard bay leaves. Carefully process with hand blender or in blender until smooth (see Safety Tip). Divide and ladle soup into 6 individual bowls. Sprinkle each with toasted seeds. Makes 6 servings.

*1 serving: 190 Calories; 2 g Total Fat (1 g Mono, .5 g Poly, 0 g Sat); 0 mg Cholesterol; 43 g Carbohydrate (6 g Fibre, 13 g Sugar); 5 g Protein; 85 mg Sodium*

**Safety Tip:** Follow manufacturer's instructions for processing hot liquids.

# Squash and Lentil Curry

*This thick, mildly spiced lentil and vegetable curry pairs well with flatbread and crisp salad.*

| | | |
|---|---|---|
| Prepared vegetable broth | 3 cups | 750 mL |
| Chopped onion | 1 1/2 cups | 375 mL |
| All-purpose flour | 2 tbsp. | 30 mL |
| Curry paste | 2 tbsp. | 30 mL |
| Garlic cloves, minced (or 1/2 tsp., 2 mL, powder) | 2 | 2 |
| Pepper | 1/4 tsp. | 1 mL |
| Chopped butternut squash | 2 cups | 500 mL |
| Canned green lentils, rinsed and drained | 1 1/4 cups | 300 mL |
| Chopped yam (or sweet potato) | 1 cup | 250 mL |
| Fresh spinach, stems removed, lightly packed | 3 cups | 750 mL |
| Frozen peas | 1 cup | 250 mL |
| Plain yogurt | 1/3 cup | 75 mL |
| Raw cashews, toasted (see Tip, page 72) | 1/3 cup | 75 mL |
| Salt, to taste | | |

Combine first 6 ingredients in inner pot.

Add squash, lentils and yam. Stir well. Cover with lid and seal. Select pressure cooker function and cook on high pressure for 8 minutes. Allow pressure to release naturally.

Add spinach and peas. Stir gently. With sauté function, cook on medium heat until spinach is wilted and peas are heated through, about 3 to 5 minutes.

Add remaining 3 ingredients. Stir gently. Makes 6 servings.

*1 serving:* 340 Calories; 8 g Total Fat (2.5 g Mono, 1 g Poly, 1.5 g Sat); 5 mg Cholesterol; 55 g Carbohydrate (10 g Fibre, 9 g Sugar); 17 g Protein; 390 mg Sodium

# Spaghetti Squash 'n' Sauce

*No more waiting for an hour for your spaghetti squash to cook in the oven! With the pressure cooker function, you can have perfectly cooked squash in minutes! The pasta-like strands of spaghetti squash offer a great low-carb alternative to traditional pasta.*

| | | |
|---|---|---|
| Small spaghetti squash (about 1 1/2 lbs., 680 g) | 1 | 1 |
| Water | 1 cup | 250 mL |
| Olive oil | 2 tsp. | 10 mL |
| Sliced fresh white mushrooms | 2 cups | 500 mL |
| Garlic cloves, minced (or 1/2 tsp., 2 mL, powder) | 2 | 2 |
| Chopped onion | 1/2 cup | 125 mL |
| Chopped red pepper | 1/2 cup | 125 mL |
| Can of diced tomatoes (14 oz., 398 mL), with juice | 1 | 1 |
| Dried thyme | 1/2 tsp. | 2 mL |
| Granulated sugar | 1/2 tsp. | 2 mL |
| Salt | 1/4 tsp. | 1 mL |
| Pepper | 1/8 tsp | 0.5 mL |
| Grated Parmesan cheese | 2 tsp. | 10 mL |

Cut squash in half lengthwise. Remove seeds. Add water and trivet to inner pot of multi-cooker and arrange squash, cut side up, on rack.
Cover with lid and seal. Select pressure cooker function and cook on high pressure for 7 minutes. Do a quick release of pressure. Transfer squash from inner pot to a plate and cover to keep warm.

Wipe out inner pot and return it to multi-cooker. With sauté function, heat olive oil on medium. Add next 4 ingredients. Cook for about 5 minutes, stirring often, until onion is softened.

Add next 5 ingredients. Cook and stir for 2 minutes to blend flavours.

Cut squash halves crosswise to make four pieces. Loosen squash strands with a fork, and transfer strands to four plates. Spoon tomato mixture over top.

Sprinkle with cheese. Makes 4 servings.

*1 serving:* 120 Calories; 4 g Total Fat (2 g Mono, 1 g Poly, 1 g Sat); 0 mg Cholesterol; 22 g Carbohydrate (4 g Fibre, 5 g Sugar); 4 g Protein; 300 mg Sodium

# Veggie Lasagna

*A rich and satisfying lasagna with plenty of vegetables and cottage cheese. You can make the sauce in the inner pot with the sauté function if you want to do all steps in the multi-pot, but it is easier to do it in a separate saucepan.*

| | | |
|---|---|---|
| Canola oil | 1 tsp. | 5 mL |
| Chopped celery | 1 cup | 250 mL |
| Chopped onion | 1 cup | 250 mL |
| Finely chopped carrot | 1 cup | 250 mL |
| Garlic cloves, minced (or 3/4 tsp., 4 mL, powder) | 3 | 3 |
| Tomato paste (see Tip, page 41) | 2 tbsp. | 30 mL |
| Grated zucchini (with peel) | 2 cups | 500 mL |
| Can of diced tomatoes (with juice) (14 oz., 398 mL) | 1 | 1 |
| Italian seasoning | 1 tbsp. | 15 mL |
| Large eggs, fork-beaten | 2 | 2 |
| Chopped fresh spinach leaves, lightly packed | 3 cups | 750 mL |
| 2% cottage cheese | 2 cups | 500 mL |
| Pepper | 1/2 tsp. | 2 mL |
| Ground nutmeg (optional) | 1/8 tsp. | 0.5 mL |
| Oven-ready whole grain lasagna noodles, broken in half | 9 | 9 |
| Water | 1 cup | 250 mL |
| Grated Italian cheese blend | 1 cup | 250 mL |

Heat canola oil in a large saucepan on medium. Add next 4 ingredients and cook for about 10 minutes, stirring often, until onion is softened.

Stir in tomato paste and cook for 1 minute. Stir in next 3 ingredients and bring to a boil, stirring occasionally. Lower heat to a simmer and let mixture reduce for about 7 minutes, stirring occasionally.

Combine next 5 ingredients in a large bowl.

Layer ingredients in a greased springform pan that fits in your multi-cooker's inner pot in the following order:

1/3 of tomato mixture, 6 noodle halves, half of spinach mixture, 1/3 of tomato mixture, 6 noodle halves, remaining spinach mixture, remaining noodle halves and remaining tomato mixture.

Cover pan with foil and place trivet in inner pot. Add water to inner pot. Use foil to make a sling and lower springform pan into inner pot. Cover with lid and seal. Select pressure cooker function and cook on high pressure for 20 minutes. Allow pressure to release naturally.

Sprinkle with Italian cheese blend. Let stand, covered, for about 3 minutes until cheese is melted. Let stand, uncovered, for 10 minutes. Makes 8 servings.

*1 serving: 220 Calories; 7 g Total Fat (2 g Mono, .5 g Poly, 3 g Sat); 45 mg Cholesterol; 23 g Carbohydrate (5 g Fibre, 6 g Sugar); 18 g Protein; 1170 mg Sodium*

# Mac 'n' Cheese

*Too hot to turn on your oven but still craving a comforting bowl of macaroni and cheese? No problem! With the pressure cooker function on your multi-cooker, you can have rich, creamy mac 'n' cheese without heating up the house, and in less time than it would take in the oven. To make clean up easier, make sure your inner pot is well greased.*

| | | |
|---|---|---|
| Water | 4 cups | 1 L |
| Package of elbow macaroni (1 lb., 454 g) | 1 | 1 |
| Butter | 1/4 cup | 60 mL |
| Dry mustard | 2 tsp. | 10 mL |
| Salt | 1 tsp. | 5 mL |
| Pepper | 1/4 tsp. | 1 mL |
| Evaporated milk | 1 cup | 250 mL |
| Grated sharp Cheddar cheese, lightly packed | 6 oz. | 170 g |
| Grated Monterey Jack cheese, lightly packed | 6 oz. | 170 g |
| Grated Pecorino Romano cheese | 1/2 cup | 125 mL |

Combine first 6 ingredients in well-greased inner pot. Cover with lid and seal. Select pressure cooker function and cook on high pressure for 4 minutes. Allow pressure to release naturally for 10 minutes and then do a quick release of any remaining pressure. If there is any excess liquid remaining in pot, use sauté function to cook for 1 to 2 minutes until liquid has evaporated. Turn off sauté function.

Add remaining 4 ingredients and stir until well mixed and creamy. Makes 7 servings.

*1 serving:* 540 Calories; 33 g Total Fat (10 g Mono, 2 g Poly, 19 g Sat); 85 mg Cholesterol; 41 g Carbohydrate (2 g Fibre, 6 g Sugar); 21 g Protein; 680 mg Sodium

# Converting Recipes for the Multi-cooker

Now that you have your multi-cooker, you are no doubt excited to capitalize on its convenience and cook as many meals with it as you can. Does that mean that your previous tried-and-true recipes and family faves are a thing of the past? Not at all. Luckily, the multi-cooker is so versatile that many recipes not written for the pressure cooker can easily be adapted to work in your multi-cooker.

The key to successfully converting a recipe is choosing a dish that is well suited to being cooked under pressure. For example, don't use the multi-cooker for foods that should be crispy, such as roasted potatoes or chicken fingers, because they won't be. Pressure cookers cannot do crispy. Moisture does not escape from the multi-cooker when it cooks under pressure, so any foods cooked in it come out moist.

When contemplating the consistency of food to expect from the cooker, think "boiled," "stewed" or "steamed" rather than "roasted" or "baked." In other words, that whole chicken you cook under pressure will come out tender and juicy, but if you are hoping for a crispy, browned skin, you'll have to toss it in the oven under the broiler for a few minutes to crisp it up.

Where the multi-cooker really shines is with big cuts of meat, such as ham, pot roasts and ribs, which typically benefit from being cooked slowly on low heat to make them tender.

It is also great for soups, stews, chili, curries…basically any soft foods that you might cook in a slow cooker. In fact, the results you get from the pressure cooker are similar to what you would get from a slow cooker (only the dish is ready in a fraction of the time). For this reason, many slow cooker recipes can easily be adapted to work in the pressure cooker.

Keep these tips in mind when converting your recipes from the slow cooker to the pressure cooker:

• For best result, recipes cooked in the multi-cooker need at least 1 cup (250 mL) of liquid; too much, though, will ruin the meal. Slow cooker recipes tend to have a lot of moisture, so either reduce the amount of liquid if possible, or use the sauté function after the pressure has been released to reduce the amount of liquid. Keep in mind, too, that the liquid does not have to come from water, wine, broth and the like. Fresh vegetables, canned tomatoes and even meat release moisture as they cook, contributing to the overall water content of a dish.

• If the recipe calls for any thickeners, such as cornstarch or flour, add them after the pressure cooking cycle has finished.

• Alcohol does not evaporate in the pressure cooker, so if you are adapting a slow cooker meal, either reduce the amount of alcohol you add, or sauté off the excess after the pressure cooking cycle.

• As a general rule, pork, beef and lamb dishes that take about 8 hours on low in a slow cooker will take from 20 to 30 minutes on high in the pressure cooker; chicken will take a little less time, from 10 to 20 minutes. For a whole chicken, we recommend 6 minutes per pound for truly succulent meat.

• Different foods need different cooking times, which can be a little tricky in the pressure cooker. For example, meat needs to cook longer than most vegetables, so if you add them to the pot together, you could end up with unpleasantly mushy vegetables. You have two options to get around this issue:

  1. Cook the meat first and then add the veggies for the last bit of cooking time, but keep in mind that it takes a while for the pressure to rise again once it has been released. OR 2. Cut the meat into smaller chunks so it will cook faster, and cut the vegetables in larger chunks so they take a bit longer to cook through.

Whichever method you choose will depend on the dish you are cooking. Experimentation is the key to mastering the multi-cooker, so have fun with it!

# Orange Mint Beets

*In this tasty side, sweet beets get a little help from tangy orange and fresh mint. If you don't want red hands, wear rubber gloves when handling beets.*

| | | |
|---|---|---|
| Water | 1 cup | 250 mL |
| Fresh medium beets, scrubbed clean and trimmed | 4 | 4 |
| Small orange, sliced | 2 | 2 |
| Chopped fresh mint (or 1/4 tsp., 1 mL, dried) | 1 tsp. | 5 mL |
| Salt, to taste | | |
| Chevre, crumbled (optional) | 1/3 cup | 75 mL |

Place trivet in bottom of inner pot and add water. Place beets on trivet. Cover with lid and seal. Select pressure cooker function and cook on high pressure for 25 minutes. Do a quick release of pressure. Let beets stand until cool enough to handle. Peel beets and cut into slices.

Arrange beets and orange slices on a platter and sprinkle with mint, salt and chevre. Makes 2 servings.

*1 serving:* 100 Calories; 0 g Total Fat (0 g Mono, 0 g Poly, 0 g Sat); 0 mg Cholesterol; 24 g Carbohydrate (4 g Fibre, 18 g Sugar); 3 g Protein; 135 mg Sodium

# Cheesy Garlic Potatoes

*A delicious mashed potato dish with added depth of flavour from the "roasted" garlic. No need to turn your oven on to roast the garlic; it goes in the multi-cooker with the potatoes for a side that is quick and fuss-free.*

| | | |
|---|---|---|
| Water | 1 cup | 250 mL |
| Garlic bulbs | 2 | 2 |
| Peeled potatoes, cut up | 3 lbs. | 1.4 kg |
| Cooking oil | 1 tbsp. | 15 mL |
| Half-and-half cream | 2/3 cup | 150 mL |
| Butter (or hard margarine) | 3 tbsp. | 45 mL |
| Finely chopped green onion | 3 tbsp. | 45 mL |
| Salt | 1 tsp. | 5 mL |
| Pepper | 1/4 tsp. | 1 mL |
| Grated havarti cheese | 1 cup | 250 mL |
| Coarsely ground pepper, for garnish | | |

Add water to inner pot. Trim 1/4 inch (6 mm) from garlic bulbs to expose tops of cloves, leaving bulbs intact. Place in steamer basket with potatoes. Cover with lid and seal. Selct pressure cooker function and cook on high pressure for 8 minutes. Do a quick release of pressure. Transfer garlic and potatoes to a large bowl and set aside until garlic is cool enough to handle. Squeeze garlic bulbs to remove cloves from skin. Discard skin. Mash garlic with a fork on a small plate. Add oil and mix until smooth.

Add next 5 ingredients and garlic to potatoes and mash.

Add cheese. Stir well. Sprinkle with pepper. Makes about 8 1/2 cups (2.1 L).

*1 cup (250 mL): 370 Calories; 20 g Total Fat (5 g Mono, 1 g Poly, 12 g Sat); 55 mg Cholesterol; 40 g Carbohydrate (4 g Fibre, 3 g Sugar); 11 g Protein; 330 mg Sodium*

# Spinach Risotto

*Nothing beats the simplicity of making risotto in the multi-cooker. You can get your dish to the table in a fraction of the time and with a fraction of the effort necessary with the stovetop method. No hovering over the pot, and no constant stirring—just set it and go do something more interesting while your multi-cooker does the work for you! Use fresh Parmesan cheese for best results.*

| | | |
|---|---|---|
| Olive (or cooking) oil | 1 tbsp. | 15 mL |
| Finely chopped onion | 1/2 cup | 125 mL |
| Arborio rice | 2 cups | 500 mL |
| Prepared vegetable broth | 4 cups | 1 L |
| Box of frozen chopped spinach (10 oz., 300 g), thawed and squeezed dry | 1 | 1 |
| Grated fresh Parmesan cheese | 1/2 cup | 125 mL |
| Chopped fresh dill | 2 tbsp. | 30 mL |

With sauté function, heat olive oil in inner pot on medium. Add onion. Cook, uncovered, for about 5 minutes, stirring often, until softened.

Add rice. Stir until coated and rice is opaque. Add broth. Turn off sauté function. Cover with lid and seal. Select pressure cooker function and cook on high pressure for 7 minutes. Do a quick release of pressure.

Add remaining 3 ingredients. Stir until heated through. Makes 10 servings.

*1 serving:* *150 Calories; 3 g Total Fat (1.5 g Mono, .5 g Poly, 1 g Sat); 5 mg Cholesterol; 26 g Carbohydrate (2 g Fibre, 2 g Sugar); 5 g Protein; 280 mg Sodium*

# Creamy Polenta

*Polenta sounds gourmet, and this creamy cornmeal dish is sure to impress your guests! Pair with ham steaks or roasted eggplant. Polenta purists might prefer to make this dish with water instead of the broth to let the corn flavour really shine through. The cream cheese is subtle, so increase it to 1/2 cup (125 mL) if you'd like a stronger cheese flavour.*

| | | |
|---|---|---|
| **Butter (or hard margarine)** | 1 tbsp. | 15 mL |
| **Prepared chicken broth** | 2 cups | 500 mL |
| **Yellow cornmeal** | 1/2 cup | 125 mL |
| **Herb and garlic cream cheese** | 1/4 cup | 60 mL |

With sauté function, melt butter in inner pot over medium heat. Add cornmeal and cook, stirring, for about 1 minute until cornmeal is coated in butter. Whisk in broth, making sure no cornmeal is stuck to the bottom or sides of pot. Turn off sauté function. Cover with lid and seal. Select pressure cooker function and cook on high pressure for 8 minutes. Allow pressure to release naturally.

Stir in cream cheese and stir until smooth. Makes about 5 cups (1.25 L).

*1 cup (250 mL):* 120 Calories; 7 g Total Fat (2 g Mono, 0 g Poly, 4 g Sat); 20 mg Cholesterol; 12 g Carbohydrate (1 g Fibre, 0 g Sugar); 4 g Protein; 290 mg Sodium

# Coconut Rice Pudding

*Creamy and comforting, sweet coconut rice contrasts with the vibrant colour of fresh mango. Dried cranberries or raisins would also be good additions.*

| | | |
|---|---|---|
| Granulated sugar | 3/4 cup | 175 mL |
| Water | 3 cups | 750 mL |
| Short-grain white rice | 2 cups | 500 mL |
| Salt | 1/4 tsp. | 1 mL |
| Can of coconut milk (14 oz., 398 mL) | 1 | 1 |
| Vanilla | 1 tsp. | 5 mL |
| Ground cinnamon | 1 tsp. | 5 mL |
| Chopped ripe (or frozen, thawed) mango | 1 1/2 cups | 375 mL |
| Medium sweetened coconut, toasted (see Tip, below) | 1/2 cup | 125 mL |

Combine sugar and water in inner pot. Stir in rice and salt. Cover with lid and seal. Select pressure cooker function and cook on high pressure for 20 minutes. Allow pressure to release naturally for 10 minutes and then do a quick release of remaining pressure.

Stir in next 4 ingredients.

Sprinkle coconut over individual servings. Makes about 7 cups (1.75 L).

*1/2 cup (125 mL): 260 Calories; 8 g Total Fat (0 g Mono, 0 g Poly, 7 g Sat); 0 mg Cholesterol; 44 g Carbohydrate (2 g Fibre, 19 g Sugar); 3 g Protein; 5 mg Sodium*

**Tip:** When toasting nuts, seeds or coconut, cooking times will vary for each type of nut—so never toast them together. For small amounts, place ingredient in an ungreased shallow frying pan. Heat on medium for 3 to 5 minutes, stirring often, until golden. For larger amounts, spread ingredient evenly in an ungreased shallow pan. Bake in a 350°F (175°C) oven for 5 to 10 minutes, stirring or shaking often, until golden.

# Decedant Cheesecake

*A perfect dessert to make when your oven is already in use. You can layer the chocolate and vanilla, or run a knife tip through the filling for a lovely marbled effect. For best results and easier mixing, make sure the cream cheese and eggs are at room temperature.*

| | | |
|---|---|---|
| Butter (or hard margarine) | 2 tbsp. | 30 mL |
| Graham cracker crumbs | 3/4 cup | 175 mL |
| Granulated sugar | 2 tsp. | 10 mL |
| Semi-sweet chocolate baking squares (1 oz., 28 g), cut up | 3 | 3 |
| Packages of light cream cheese (8 oz., 225 g), softened | 2 | 2 |
| Granulated sugar | 1/2 cup | 125 mL |
| Plain Greek yogurt | 1/3 cup | 75 mL |
| Vanilla | 1/2 tsp. | 2 mL |
| Large eggs, room temperature | 2 | 2 |
| All-purpose flour | 2 tsp. | 10 mL |
| Water | 1 1/2 cups | 375 mL |

For the crust, melt butter in a saucepan. Stir in graham crumbs and first amount of sugar. Press in ungreased springform pan that will fit into the inner pot of your multi-cooker.

For the filling, melt chocolate in a saucepan over low, stirring often. Beat cream cheese, remaining sugar, yogurt and vanilla together in a large bowl until smooth. Beat in eggs, 1 at a time, mixing until just combined. Mix in flour. Reserve 1 1/4 cups (300 mL) of cheese mixture. Pour remaining cheese mixture over bottom crust. Stir melted chocolate into reserved cheese mixture and pour over top of white layer. Cover pan with foil.

Tear off a 16 inch (40 cm) long piece of foil to make a foil strap. Fold lengthwise to make a strip 16 inches (40 cm) long and 4 inches (10 cm) wide. Set cake pan on center of foil strap. Put wire trivet in bottom of inner pot. Add water. Using foil strap, carefully lower pan into inner pot, leaving foil strap in pot to use to remove pan when baking is complete. Select pressure cooker function and cook on high pressure for 37 minutes. Allow pressure to release naturally for 20 minutes and then do a quick release of any remaining pressure. Use foil strap to remove pan from inner pot. Remove foil and let cool to room temperature on a wire rack. Refrigerate for several hours or overnight. Cuts into 12 wedges.

*1 wedge:* 260 Calories; 19 g Total Fat (4.5 g Mono, 1 g Poly, 11 g Sat); 70 mg Cholesterol; 20 g Carbohydrate (0 g Fibre, 15 g Sugar); 5 g Protein; 170 mg Sodium

# The Slow Cooker

When you consider that the meals you cook in the pressure cooker and the slow cooker are comparable in taste and texture, you might wonder why you would ever choose the slow cooker over the pressure cooker. Why wait hours for your meal to cook when you can cook it under pressure and have dinner on the table in a fraction of the time?

Well, it depends, in part, how organized you are with your meal planning. The pressure cooker is fast, but it is not instant. Even if you do the prep work in advance, with the pressure cooker you still have to cook the dish when you get home, which means waiting for the pressure to build, the food to cook and the pressure to release before you can eat. With the slow cooker, however, you can set everything up before you leave the house in the morning and come home to a meal that is ready to eat as soon as you walk through the door.

Another advantage of the slow cooker is that that you can adjust your recipe as it cooks. With the pressure cooker, especially with an untried recipe, you basically toss in the ingredients and hope for the best. With the slow cooker, you can fiddle with seasoning as the food cooks, making adjustments throughout the cooking process to ensure the end result will be to your liking.

When choosing which recipes to cook with your multi-cooker's slow cooker function, keep the following tips in mind:

• Frozen meat should not be cooked with the slow cooker function. Because slow cooker temperatures are so low, the meat may stay at the temperature "danger zone" for too long, which could allow bacteria to multiply and ultimately lead to food poisoning.

• In most cases, it is a good idea to brown your meat before starting the slow cooking process. Not only does the browning step improve the overall flavour of the dish, it also allows some of the fat to be rendered and drained so your finished product is not greasy.

• Milk products tend not to fare well in the slow cooker and should be added near the end of the cooking time.

• Pasta and rice should either be added near the end of the cooking time or cooked in a separate pot and added to the dish just before serving to prevent them from becoming mushy or gummy.

• Hardy vegetables, such as sweet potatoes or other root vegetables, can be added early on, but delicate vegetables such as summer squash and peppers should be added in the last 30 or so minutes of cooking time so they maintain some textural integrity (i.e. not mush).

# Beef and Beer Stew

*The beer connoisseur will be glad to know that this hearty beef, beer and barley stew goes marvellously well with...beer!*

| | | |
|---|---|---|
| Canola oil | 2 tsp. | 10 mL |
| Stewing beef, trimmed of fat, cut into 3/4 inch (2 cm) pieces | 2 lbs. | 900 g |
| Bottle of brown ale or stout (14 oz. 398 mL) | 1 | 1 |
| Prepared beef broth | 1 cup | 250 mL |
| Water | 1 cup | 250 mL |
| Brown sugar, packed | 2 tbsp. | 30 mL |
| Dijon mustard | 1 tbsp. | 15 mL |
| Chili powder | 2 tsp. | 10 mL |
| Dried thyme | 1/2 tsp. | 2 mL |
| Salt | 1/2 tsp. | 2 mL |
| Pepper | 1/4 tsp. | 1 mL |
| Pot barley | 1/2 cup | 125 mL |
| Thinly sliced onion | 1 cup | 250 mL |
| Chopped carrot | 1 cup | 250 mL |
| Chopped celery | 1 cup | 250 mL |
| Garlic cloves, minced (or 1/2 tsp., 2 mL, powder) | 2 | 2 |
| Chopped fresh parsley (optional) | 2 tbsp. | 30 mL |

With sauté function, heat canola oil in inner pot on high. Cook beef, in 2 batches, for 3 to 5 minutes, stirring occasionally, until browned. Remove from pot and set aside.

Stir next 9 ingredients into inner pot, scraping any brown bits from bottom of pan. Turn off sauté function. Add beef and next 5 ingredients to inner pot. Cover with lid ensuring pressure release is in venting position. Select slow cooker function and cook on low for 8 to 9 hours or on high for 4 to 4 1/2 hours.

Sprinkle with parsley. Makes about 7 1/2 cups (1.9 L).

*1 cup (250 mL):* 380 Calories; 13 g Total Fat (5 g Mono, 1 g Poly, 4.5 g Sat); 100 mg Cholesterol; 19 g Carbohydrate (2 g Fibre, 5 g Sugar); 42 g Protein; 320 mg Sodium

# Meat Sauce

*With just the right amount of spice, this is a meat sauce the whole family will love. Serve with your favourite long pasta, such as spaghetti or linguini.*

| | | |
|---|---|---|
| Lean ground beef | 1 lb. | 454 g |
| Medium onions, chopped | 2 | 2 |
| Celery ribs, chopped | 2 | 2 |
| Medium green pepper, chopped (optional) | 1 | 1 |
| Garlic clove, minced (or 1/4 tsp., 1 mL, powder) | 1 | 1 |
| Can of crushed tomatoes (14 oz., 398 mL) | 1 | 1 |
| Can of diced tomatoes (28 oz., 796 mL), with juice | 1 | 1 |
| Water | 1/3 cup | 75 mL |
| Chopped fresh parsley (or 2 1/2 tsp., 12 mL, flakes) | 3 tbsp. | 45 mL |
| Dried whole oregano | 1 tsp. | 5 mL |
| Bay leaf | 1 | 1 |
| Chopped fresh sweet basil (or 3/4 tsp., 4 mL, dried) | 1 tbsp. | 15 mL |
| Salt | 1/2 tsp. | 2 mL |
| Granulated sugar | 1/2 tsp. | 2 mL |
| Dried crushed chilies | 1 tsp. | 5 mL |
| Freshly ground pepper, sprinkle | | |

Grated Parmesan cheese, for garnish

With sauté function, scramble-fry ground beef, onion, celery, green pepper and garlic in inner pot on medium until beef is no longer pink. Turn off sauté function and drain fat.

Stir in next 11 ingredients. Cover with lid ensuring pressure release valve is in venting position. Select slow cooker function and cook on low for 6 to 7 hours or on high for 3 to 3 1/2 hours. Remove and discard bay leaf.

Garnish individual servings with Parmesan cheese. Makes 6 servings.

*1 serving:* 270 Calories; 11 g Total Fat (4.5 g Mono, 0.5 g Poly, 4.5 g Sat); 65 mg Cholesterol; 18 g Carbohydrate (4 g Fibre, 10 g Sugar); 26 g Protein; 700 mg Sodium

# Beef Hot Pot

*A mildly spicy hot pot cooked with the slow cooker function of your multi-cooker. A good dose of vegetables offers plenty of colour and texture. Freeze leftovers in individual portions and reheat in the microwave for convenient last-minute meals.*

| | | |
|---|---|---|
| Cooking oil | 2 tbsp | 30 mL |
| Stewing beef, trimmed of fat, cut into 3/4 inch (2 cm) pieces | 1 1/2 lbs. | 680 g |
| Prepared beef broth | 3 cups | 750 mL |
| Sliced carrot | 2 cups | 500 mL |
| Sliced fresh shiitake mushrooms | 2 cups | 500 mL |
| Can of cut baby corn (14 oz., 398 mL), drained | 1 | 1 |
| Can of shoestring-style bamboo shoots (8 oz., 227 mL), drained | 1 | 1 |
| Chopped onion | 1 cup | 250 mL |
| Water | 1 cup | 250 mL |
| Finely grated ginger root (or 1/2 tsp., 2 mL, ground ginger) | 2 tsp. | 10 mL |
| Chili paste (sambal oelek) | 1 tsp. | 5 mL |
| Garlic clove, minced (or 1/4 tsp., 1 mL, powder) | 1 | 1 |
| Chopped fresh spinach leaves, lightly packed | 1 cup | 250 mL |
| Sliced trimmed sugar snap peas | 1 cup | 250 mL |
| Sliced green onion | 3 tbsp. | 45 mL |
| Rice vinegar | 1 tbsp. | 15 mL |
| Soy sauce | 1 tbsp. | 15 mL |
| Sesame oil (for flavour) | 1 tsp. | 5 mL |
| Salt | 1/4 tsp. | 1 mL |

With sauté function, heat canola oil in inner pot on high. Cook beef, in 2 batches, for 3 to 5 minutes, stirring occasionally, until browned. Turn off sauté function.

Combine next 10 ingredients in inner pot. Cover with lid ensuring pressure release valve is in venting position. Select slow cooker function and cook on low for 8 to 10 hours or on high for 4 1/2 to 5 hours.

Stir in remaining 7 ingredients. Let stand, covered, for 10 minutes. Makes about 10 cups (2.5 L).

*1 cup (250 mL):* 220 Calories; 5 g Total Fat (2 g Mono, .5 g Poly, 1.5 g Sat); 55 mg Cholesterol; 18 g Carbohydrate (3 g Fibre, 5 g Sugar); 26 g Protein; 570 mg Sodium

# Slow Cooker Fajitas

*Serve the tender, spiced beef and veggies wrapped in corn or flour tortillas with your favourite toppings, such as avocado, tomato, lettuce, sour cream and cheese*

| | | |
|---|---|---|
| **Beef sirloin tip steak, sliced into 3 inch (7.5 cm) thin strips** | 1 1/2 lbs. | 680 g |
| **Thickly sliced fresh white mushrooms** | 2 cups | 500 mL |
| **Red medium pepper, cut into 1/2 inch (12 mm) wide strips** | 1 | 1 |
| **Canned kernel corn (7 oz., 199 mL)** | 1 | 1 |
| **Large onion, cut lengthwise into 8 wedges** | 1 | 1 |
| **Finely chopped pickled jalapeño peppers, drained (optional)** | 1 tbsp. | 15 mL |
| **Package of fajita seasoning mix (1 oz., 28 g)** | 1 | 1 |
| **Water** | 1/4 cup | 60 mL |

Place first 6 ingredients in inner pot.

Combine seasoning mix and water in a small dish and add to inner pot. Cover with lid ensuring pressure release valve is in venting postition. Select slow cooker function and cook on low for 5 to 6 hours or on high for 2 1/2 to 3 hours until beef is tender. Strain beef and vegetables, reserving liquid for another purpose. Use about 1/2 cup (125 mL) beef mixture per tortilla. Makes 10 servings.

*1 serving: 130 Calories; 3 g Total Fat (1 g Mono, 0 g Poly, 1 g Sat); 45 mg Cholesterol; 6 g Carbohydrate (0 g Fibre, 2 g Sugar); 20 g Protein; 290 mg Sodium*

# Meatballs in Pineapple Sauce

*This pineapple sauce, infused with chili and lime, adds an exotic flair to meatballs. A dominant ginger flavour makes this dish particularly delicious!*

| | | |
|---|---|---|
| Cooking oil | 1 tbsp. | 15 mL |
| Finely chopped onion | 1/3 cup | 75 mL |
| Finely grated, peeled ginger root | 2 tsp. | 10 mL |
| Can of pineapple tidbits (14 oz., 398 mL), drained and juice reserved | 1 | 1 |
| Sweet chili sauce | 1/2 cup | 125 mL |
| Lime juice | 3 tbsp. | 45 mL |
| Minced crystallized ginger | 1 tbsp. | 15 mL |
| Soy sauce | 2 tsp. | 10 mL |
| Salt | 1/4 tsp. | 1 mL |
| Pre-cooked meatballs | 36 | 36 |
| Reserved pineapple juice | 2/3 cup | 150 mL |
| Cornstarch | 2 tsp. | 10 mL |
| Grated lime zest | 1/4 tsp. | 1 mL |

With sauté function, heat cooking oil in inner pot on medium. Add onion and cook for about 2 minutes, stirring often, until starting to soften. Add ginger. Cook, stirring, for another 2 to 3 minutes until onion is softened. Turn off sauté function.

Stir in next 6 ingredients.

Add meatballs and stir until coated. Cover with lid ensuring pressure release valve is in venting position. Select slow cooker function and cook on Low for 5 to 7 hours or high for 2 to 3 hours.

Stir reserved pineapple juice and cornstarch in small bowl until smooth. Slowly add to crushed pineapple mixture, stirring constantly. With sauté function, cook on medium heat, stirring constantly, for 2 to 3 minutes until boiling and slightly thickened. Turn off sauté function. Stir in lime zest. Makes 6 servings.

*1 serving: 370 Calories; 8 g Total Fat (1.5 g Mono, .5 g Poly, 8 g Sat); 45 mg Cholesterol; 28 g Carbohydrate (2 g Fibre, 20 g Sugar); 11 g Protein; 810 mg Sodium*

# Sous Vide

A fairly recent addition to some higher-end multi-cooker models is the sous vide function. Sous vide is not a new cooking technique; it has been a staple in the kitchens of many high-end restaurants for years. And now, thanks to appliances like the multi-cooker with a sous vide option, this technique is gaining popularity with the home cook as well.

Sous vide cooking involves placing your food in a vacuum-sealed bag and immersing it in water; the temperature of the water determines how much the food cooks, and the food will not burn or overcook because the

internal temperature of the food will not rise above the temperature you set. Because the temperatures are so low, the food cooks slowly and for a longer time than with the other more conventional methods, such as frying or grilling. Even though it cooks for longer, the food is more nutritious than items cooked in more traditional ways because fewer nutrients are destroyed by the low temperatures and none are lost to the water that cooks the food, unlike with boiling or steaming.

Foods that are cooked sous vide come out tender and moist, but they do not brown. Some foods, such as many cuts of meat, can be finished with a "reverse sear" (i.e. the food is seared after it is fully cooked rather than before) in a frying pan once the sous vide cooking cycle is complete to give it a that brown, caramelized crust.

Here are some things to keep in mind should you decide to give sous vide cooking a try:

- Temperature of food items should be no higher than 43°F (6°C) when they are added to the bag, or the texture of the end result could be compromised. Basically, you want your food to be the temperature it would be coming out of your fridge.

- Make sure you get as much air out of the bag as possible so the water makes better contact with the food.

- The food must stay submerged in the water to cook properly.

- The thickness of the food matters more than its overall size, meaning a 1 inch (2.5 cm) thick steak will need less time than a steak that is 2 inches (5 cm) thick.

- Many types of vegetables work well cooked sous vide. Root vegetables such as carrots, sweet potatoes and beets, fare the best, but you can also cook Brussels sprouts, asparagus, broccoli, artichokes and many others.

| Food | Thickness | Temperature | Time (minimum) | Time (maximum) |
|------|-----------|-------------|----------------|----------------|
| **Beef** | | | | |
| Tenderloin, sirloin, rib-eye, t-bone | 1 inch (2.5 cm) | 134°F (57°C) or higher | 1 hour | 4 hours |
| Spare ribs | 2 inch (5 cm) | 134°F (57°C) or higher | 24 hours | 48 to 72 hours |
| Flank steak | 1 inch (2.5 cm) | 134°F (57°C) or higher | 8 hours | 24 hours |
| Brisket | 2 inch (5 cm) | 134°F (57°C) or higher | 8 hours | 24 hours |
| **Pork** | | | | |
| Chops, cutlets, tenderloin | 1 inch (2.5 cm) | 134°F (57°C) or higher | 1.5 hours | 6 to 8 hours |
| Roast | 2.75 inch (7 cm) | 160°F (71°C) to 176°F (80°C) | 12 hours | 30 hours |
| Spare ribs | 2 inch (5 cm) | 160°F (71°C) to 176°F (80°C) | 12 hours | 30 hours |
| Baby back ribs | 1 inch (2.5 cm) | 165°F (74°C) | 4 to 8 hours | 12 hours |
| **Lamb** | | | | |
| Lambchops | 1 inch (2.5 cm) | 134°F (57°C) or higher | 1 hour | 4 hours |
| Roast | 2.75 inch (7 cm) | 134°F (57°C) or higher | 12 hours | 30 hours |
| **Poultry** | | | | |
| Chicken breast, bone in | 2 inch (5 cm) | 146°F (63°C) or higher | 2.5 hours | 4 to 6 hours |
| Chicken Breast, boneless | 1 inch (2.5 cm) | 146°F (63°C) or higher | 1 hour | 2 to 4 hours |
| Chicken leg or thigh, bone-in | | 165°F (74°C) to 176°F (80°C) | 4 hours | 6 to 8 hours |
| Chicken thigh, boneless | 1 inch (2.5 cm) | 165°F (74°C) to 176°F (80°C) | 2 hours | 4 to 6 hours |
| **Vegetables** | | | | |
| Root vegetables | Up to 1 inch (2.5 cm) | 183°F (84°C) | 1 to 2 hours | 4 hours |
| Asparagus, broccoli, cauliflower, green beans | Up to 1 inch (2.5 cm) | 183°F (84°C) | 30 minutes | 1.5 hours |
| **Eggs** | | | | |
| Soft-cooked (in shell) | Large | 146°F (63°C) | 45 minutes | 1.5 hours |
| Hard-cooked (in shell) | Large | 160°F (71°C) | 45 minutes | 1.5 hours |
| Scrambled (6 eggs) | large | 165°F (74°C) | 20 minutes | 30 minutes |

**Note:** The times listed above are specifically intended for multi-cookers with a sous vide function. They should not be used in a multi-cooker that does not have the sous vide option unless an immersion circulator is also used.

# Sassy Sauce

*Red wine and spicy Italian sausage add a ton of sass to the gentle sweetness of squash. Serve this slow cooker sauce with multi-coloured fettuccine for a truly stylish supper.*

| | | |
|---|---|---|
| Cooking oil | 2 tsp. | 10 mL |
| Italian sausage, casing removed | 1 1/2 lb. | 680 g |
| Garlic cloves, minced (or 1/2 tsp., 2 mL, powder) | 2 | 2 |
| Can of crushed tomatoes (28 oz., 796 mL) | 1 | 1 |
| Chopped butternut squash | 2 1/2 cups | 625 mL |
| Chopped celery | 2 cups | 500 mL |
| Chopped onion | 2 cups | 500 mL |
| Can of tomato sauce (14 oz., 398 mL) | 1 | 1 |
| Dry (or alcohol-free) red wine | 1 cup | 250 mL |
| Dried oregano | 1 tsp. | 5 mL |
| Dried basil | 1/2 tsp. | 2 mL |
| Bay leaf | 1 | 1 |
| Salt | 1/4 tsp. | 1 mL |
| Pepper | 1/2 tsp. | 2 mL |

With sauté function, heat cooking oil in inner pot on medium. Add sausage and garlic. Scramble-fry for about 5 minutes until browned. Turn off sauté function and drain.

Stir in remaining 11 ingredients. Cover with lid ensuring pressure release valve is in venting position. Select slow cooker function and cook on low for 8 to 10 hours or on high for 4 to 5 hours. Remove and discard bay leaf. Store in airtight container in refrigerator for up to 5 days or in freezer for up to 3 months. Makes about 9 cups (2.25 L).

*1 cup (250 mL): 370 Calories; 25 g Total Fat (11 g Mono, 3.5 g Poly, 9 g Sat); 55 mg Cholesterol; 19 g Carbohydrate (3 g Fibre, 8 g Sugar); 13 g Protein; 990 mg Sodium*

# Artichoke Pork Stew

*Tangy artichoke really comes through in this thick, savoury stew. Potatoes, pork and mushrooms add not only flavour but also a satisfying texture. Serve with salad and crusty bread to make it a complete meal.*

| | | |
|---|---|---|
| Olive oil | 1 tsp. | 5 mL |
| Boneless pork shoulder blade roast, trimmed of fat and cut into 1 inch (2.5 cm) pieces | 2 lbs. | 900 g |
| Olive oil | 2 tsp. | 10 mL |
| Chopped fresh brown (or white) mushrooms | 2 cups | 500 mL |
| Chopped leek (white part only) | 2 cups | 500 mL |
| Garlic cloves, minced (or 1/2 tsp., 2 mL, powder) | 2 | 2 |
| Dried oregano | 1 tsp. | 5 mL |
| All-purpose flour | 2 tbsp. | 30 mL |
| Prepared vegetable broth | 3 cups | 750 mL |
| Chopped peeled potato | 2 cups | 500 mL |
| Jar of marinated artichoke hearts (6 oz., 170 mL), drained and chopped | 1 | 1 |
| Salt | 1/2 tsp. | 2 mL |
| Pepper | 1/2 tsp. | 2 mL |
| Lemon juice | 1 tbsp. | 15 mL |

With sauté function, heat first amount of olive oil in inner pot on high. Add pork. Cook for about 4 minutes, stirring occasionally, until browned. Transfer to a bowl. Reduce heat to medium.

Heat second amount of olive oil in inner pot. Add next 4 ingredients and cook for about 10 minutes, stirring occasionally, until mushrooms are browned.

Sprinkle with flour. Heat, stirring, for 1 minute. Slowly add broth, stirring constantly. Heat and stir, scraping any brown bits from bottom of pan, until boiling and thickened. Turn off sauté function.

Stir in next 4 ingredients and pork. Cover with lid ensuring pressure release valve is in venting position. Select slow cooker function and cook on low 8 to 10 hours or on high for 4 1/2 to 5 hours.

Stir in lemon juice. Makes about 6 cups (1.5 L).

*1 cup (250 mL): 470 Calories; 23 g Total Fat (11 g Mono, 2 g Poly, 8 g Sat); 135 mg Cholesterol; 22 g Carbohydrate (3 g Fibre, 5 g Sugar); 43 g Protein; 690 mg Sodium*

# Hot and Spicy Pork

*The slow cooker function on your multi-cooker is perfect for cooking this pork and yam dish. Serve with rice or noodles.*

| | | |
|---|---|---|
| All-purpose flour | 3 tbsp. | 45 mL |
| Pork shoulder butt roast or steaks, trimmed of fat and cut into 3/4 inch (2 cm) pieces | 2 lbs. | 900 g |
| Cooking oil | 1 tbsp. | 15 mL |
| Ground cumin | 1 tsp. | 5 mL |
| Paprika | 1 tsp. | 5 mL |
| Ground turmeric | 1 tsp. | 5 mL |
| Prepared chicken broth | 1 1/2 cups | 375 mL |
| Chili paste (sambal oelek) | 1 tbsp. | 15 mL |
| Salt | 1/4 tsp. | 1 mL |
| Chopped onion | 1 cup | 250 mL |
| Chopped carrot | 1 cup | 250 mL |
| Yams (or sweet potatoes), peeled, cut into 1/2 inch (12 mm) pieces | 1 lb. | 454 g |
| Chopped fresh cilantro or parsley (or 1 1/2 tsp., 7 mL, dried) | 2 tbsp. | 30 mL |
| Sour cream | 2 tbsp. | 30 mL |

Measure flour into a large resealable freezer bag. Add 1/2 of pork. Seal bag and toss until coated. Repeat with remaining pork. With sauté function, heat cooking oil in inner pot on medium. Add pork in 2 batches. Cook for 5 to 10 minutes per batch, stirring occasionally, until browned. Transfer to a large plate or bowl.

Add cumin, paprika and turmeric to inner pot. Heat, stirring, for about 1 minute until fragrant. Slowly add broth, stirring constantly and scraping any brown bits from bottom of pan. Add chili paste and salt. Heat, stirring, for 1 to 2 minutes until hot. Turn off sauté function. Add onion, carrot and pork. Cover with lid ensuring pressure release valve is in venting position. Select slow cooker function and cook on low for 8 to 10 hours or on high for 4 to 5 hours.

Add yam. Stir well. Cover with lid ensuring pressure release valve is in venting position. Cook on high for about 45 minutes until yam is tender. Turn off slow cooker function.

Add cilantro and sour cream. Stir well. Makes 8 servings.

*1 serving: 390 Calories; 16 g Total Fat (7 g Mono, 2 g Poly, 5 g Sat); 100 mg Cholesterol; 24 g Carbohydrate (4 g Fibre, 3 g Sugar); 37 g Protein; 510 mg Sodium*

# Oaxacan Lamb Shanks

*The sauce is reminiscent of the mild but complex orangey-red Mole Coloradito, one of the seven moles of Oaxaca. The more traditional plantain has been replaced with sweet potato. Serve with rice.*

| | | |
|---|---|---|
| Cooking oil | 1 tsp. | 5 mL |
| Lamb shanks (about 3 1/2 lbs., 1.6 kg), trimmed of fat | 6 | 6 |
| Peeled orange-fleshed sweet potato, cut in 1 inch (2.5 cm) pieces (about 1 lb., 454 g) | 4 cups | 1 L |
| Water | 2 cups | 500 mL |
| Can of tomato paste (5 1/2 oz., 156 mL) | 1 | 1 |
| Envelope of taco seasoning mix (1 1/4 oz., 35 g) | 1 | 1 |
| Cocoa, sifted if lumpy | 1 tbsp. | 15 mL |
| Cinnamon stick (4 inches, 10 cm) | 1 | 1 |
| Salsa verde (tomatillo salsa) | 2 tbsp. | 30 mL |

With sauté function, heat cooking oil in inner pot on high. Add lamb shanks and cook for about 8 minutes, turning occasionally, until browned on all sides. Turn off sauté function. Add sweet potato.

Stir next 4 ingredients in a medium bowl until smooth. Pour over sweet potato. Add cinnamon stick. Cover with lid ensuring pressure release valve is in venting position. Select slow cooker function and cook on low for 8 to 10 hours or on high for 4 1/2 to 5 hours. Transfer lamb shanks to a serving bowl. Cover to keep warm.

Remove and discard cinnamon stick. Skim and discard fat from cooking liquid. Following manufacturer's instructions for processing hot liquids, carefully process cooking liquid with a hand blender or blender in batches until smooth. Stir in salsa. Pour over lamb. Makes 6 servings.

*1 serving: 670 Calories; 37 g Total Fat (15 g Mono, 3 g Poly, 16 g Sat); 180 mg Cholesterol; 30 g Carbohydrate (4 g Fibre, 13 g Sugar); 53 g Protein; 580 mg Sodium*

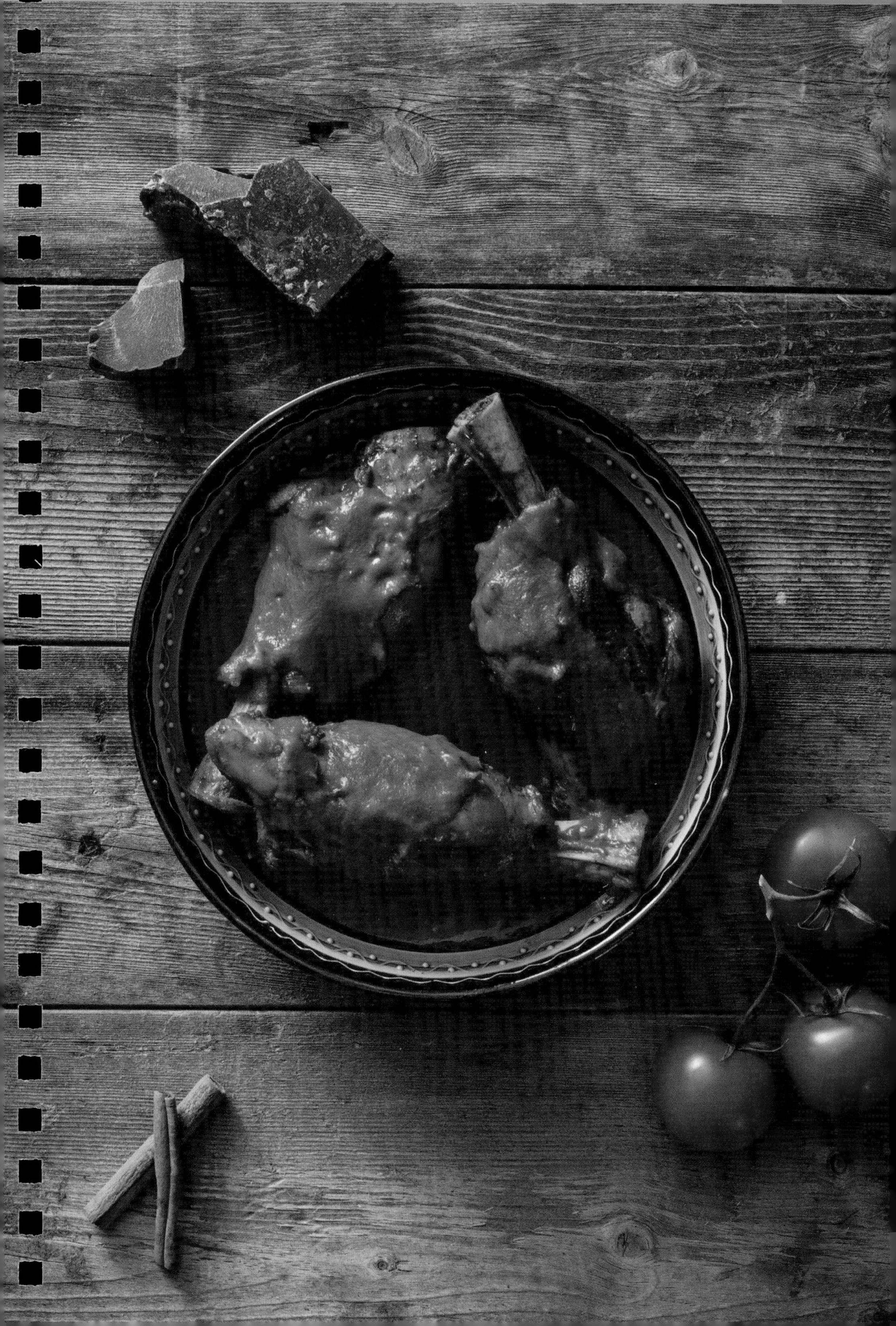

# Lamb Tagine

*This rich and sweet lamb stew packs a pleasantly spicy heat and is made with the convenience of the slow cooker function of your multi-cooker. It's perfect for the buffet table.*

| | | |
|---|---|---|
| All-purpose flour | 3 tbsp. | 45 mL |
| Salt | 1/2 tsp. | 2 mL |
| Pepper | 1/4 tsp. | 1 mL |
| Boneless lamb shoulder, trimmed of fat and cut into 1 1/2 inch (3.8 cm) pieces | 3 lbs. | 1.4 kg |
| Cooking oil | 2 tbsp. | 30 mL |
| Cooking oil | 2 tsp. | 10 mL |
| Chopped onion | 2 cups | 500 mL |
| Brown sugar, packed | 2 tsp. | 10 mL |
| Garlic cloves, minced | 2 | 2 |
| Ground ginger | 1 1/2 tsp. | 7 mL |
| Ground cinnamon | 1 tsp. | 5 mL |
| Ground allspice | 3/4 tsp. | 4 mL |
| Dried crushed chilies | 1/2 tsp. | 2 mL |
| Prepared beef broth | 2 cups | 500 mL |
| Dried apricots, halved | 1 cup | 250 mL |
| Sun-dried tomatoes, softened in boiling water for 10 minutes before chopping | 1/2 cup | 125 mL |

Combine first 3 ingredients in large resealable freezer bag. Add half of lamb. Seal bag. Toss until coated. Transfer lamb to a plate. Repeat with remaining lamb. Discard any remaining flour mixture. With sauté function, heat first amount of cooking oil in inner pot on high. Cook lamb, in 2 batches, for about 4 minutes, stirring occasionally, until browned. Transfer to a large plate or bowl. Reduce heat to medium.

Heat second amount of cooking oil in inner pot. Add onion and cook for about 5 minutes, stirring often, until onion starts to soften.

Add next 6 ingredients. Heat, stirring, for about 2 minutes until garlic is fragrant. Add broth. Heat, stirring and scraping any brown bits from bottom of pan, until boiling. Turn off sauté function. Add lamb and scatter apricots and tomatoes over top. Cover with lid ensuring pressure release valve is in venting position. Select slow cooker function and cook on low for 8 to 10 hours or on high for 4 to 5 hours. Makes about 5 cups (1.25 L).

*1 cup (250 mL): 980 Calories; 57 g Total Fat (24 g Mono, 6 g Poly, 23 g Sat); 255 mg Cholesterol; 45 g Carbohydrate (6 g Fibre, 27 g Sugar); 70 g Protein; 830 mg Sodium*

# Harvest Chicken Chili

*A thick chicken chili that will please traditionalists, yet offers special appeal to the adventurous. Sweet corn, cranberries and spinach add real personality to this dish.*

| | | |
|---|---|---|
| Cooking oil | 2 tsp. | 10 mL |
| Lean ground chicken | 1 1/2 lbs. | 680 g |
| Chopped onion | 1 cup | 250 mL |
| Chili powder | 2 tbsp. | 30 mL |
| Garlic clove, minced (or 1/4 tsp., 1 mL, powder) | 1 | 1 |
| Ground cumin | 1 tsp. | 5 mL |
| Salt | 3/4 tsp. | 4 mL |
| Can of diced tomatoes (28 oz., 796 mL), with juice | 1 | 1 |
| Can of black beans (19 oz., 540 mL), rinsed and drained | 1 | 1 |
| Cubed butternut squash (3/4 inch, 2 cm, pieces) | 1 1/2 cups | 375 mL |
| Kernel corn | 1/2 cup | 125 mL |
| Prepared chicken broth | 1/2 cup | 125 mL |
| Tomato paste (see Tip, page 41) | 2 tbsp. | 30 mL |
| Ketchup | 1 tbsp. | 15 mL |
| Chopped fresh spinach leaves, lightly packed | 2 cups | 500 mL |
| Dried cranberries | 1/2 cup | 125 mL |

With sauté function, heat cooking oil in inner pot on medium. Add chicken and scramble-fry for about 5 minutes until no longer pink.

Add next 5 ingredients and cook for about 5 minutes, stirring often, until onion is softened. Turn off sauté function.

Stir in next 7 ingredients. Cover with lid ensuring pressure release valve is in venting position. Select slow cooker function and cook on low for 6 to 7 hours or on high for 3 to 3 1/2 hours.

Stir in spinach and cranberries. Makes about 9 1/2 cups (2.4 L).

*1 cup (250 mL):* 410 Calories; 12 g Total Fat (1 g Mono, 1 g Poly, 0 g Sat); 60 mg Cholesterol; 49 g Carbohydrate (12 g Fibre, 8 g Sugar); 30 g Protein; 530 mg Sodium

# Rustic Turkey Stew

*This hearty stew is loaded with tender turkey and vegetables in a rich-tasting, smoky gravy. Serve with fresh crusty rolls or garlic bread.*

| | | |
|---|---|---|
| All-purpose flour | 1/2 cup | 125 mL |
| Salt | 1/2 tsp. | 2 mL |
| Pepper | 1/2 tsp. | 2 mL |
| Boneless, skinless turkey thighs, cut into 2 inch (5 cm) pieces | 1 lb. | 454 g |
| Bacon slices, diced | 3 | 3 |
| Cooking oil | 1 tbsp. | 15 mL |
| Cooking oil | 2 tsp. | 10 mL |
| Sliced fresh white mushrooms | 2 cups | 500 mL |
| Chopped onion | 1 cup | 250 mL |
| Garlic clove, minced (or 1/4 tsp., 1 mL, powder) | 1 | 1 |
| Dry (or alcohol-free) white wine | 1/2 cup | 125 mL |
| Prepared chicken broth | 2 1/2 cups | 625 mL |
| Baby potatoes, larger ones cut in half | 1 lb. | 454 g |
| Sliced carrot | 1 cup | 250 mL |
| Sliced celery | 1 cup | 250 mL |
| Bay leaf | 1 | 1 |

Combine first 3 ingredients in a large resealable freezer bag. Add half of turkey. Seal bag and toss until coated. Transfer turkey to a plate. Repeat with remaining turkey. Reserve any remaining flour mixture. Set aside.

With sauté function, cook bacon in inner pot on medium until crisp. Transfer with a slotted spoon to a plate lined with paper towel to drain. Discard drippings.

Heat first amount of cooking oil in inner pot on high. Add turkey and cook for about 5 minutes, stirring occasionally, until browned. Transfer to a large plate. Reduce heat to medium.

Add next 4 ingredients and cook for 5 to 10 minutes, stirring often, until onion is softened. Sprinkle with reserved flour mixture. Heat, stirring, for 1 minute.

Slowly add wine, stirring constantly and scraping any brown bits from bottom of pan. Stir in broth. Turn off sauté function.

Stir in bacon, turkey and next 3 ingredients. Add bay leaf. Cover with lid ensuring pressure release valve is in venting position. Select slow cooker function and cook on low for 6 to 7 hours or on high for 3 to 3 1/2 hours. Discard bay leaf. Makes 4 servings.

*1 serving:* 570 Calories; 26 g Total Fat (15 g Mono, 6 g Poly, 10 g Sat); 115 mg Cholesterol; 46 g Carbohydrate (5 g Fibre, 6 g Sugar); 34 g Protein; 610 mg Sodium

# Cajun Chicken and Barley

*Experience the spicy flavours of the Louisiana bayou with this spicy tomato, chicken and barley dish.*

| | | |
|---|---|---|
| Canola oil | 1 tsp. | 5 mL |
| Hot Italian sausage, casing removed, chopped | 1/2 lb. | 225 g |
| Boneless, skinless chicken thighs, halved | 1 1/4 lbs. | 560 g |
| Can of diced tomatoes (14 oz., 398 mL), with juice | 1 | 1 |
| Chopped green pepper | 1 1/2 cups | 375 mL |
| Chopped celery | 1 cup | 250 mL |
| Chopped onion | 1 cup | 250 mL |
| Prepared chicken broth | 1 cup | 250 mL |
| Can of tomato sauce (7 1/2 oz., 213 mL) | 1 | 1 |
| Pot barley | 1/2 cup | 125 mL |
| Cajun seasoning | 2 tsp. | 10 mL |
| Garlic cloves, minced (or 1/2 tsp., 2 mL, powder) | 2 | 2 |

With sauté function, heat canola oil in inner pot on medium. Add sausage and scramble-fry for about 5 minutes until starting to brown. Transfer with a slotted spoon to a plate lined with paper towel to drain. Turn off sauté function.

Add chicken to inner pot. Combine remaining 9 ingredients in a large bowl and pour over chicken. Stir in sausage. Cover with lid ensuring pressure release valve is in venting position. Select slow cooker function and cook on low for 7 to 8 hours or on high for 3 1/2 to 4 hours until barley is tender. Makes about 9 cups (2.25 L).

*1 cup (250 mL): 230 Calories; 12 g Total Fat (4 g Mono, 1.5 g Poly, 3 g Sat); 45 mg Cholesterol; 16 g Carbohydrate (3 g Fibre, 5 g Sugar); 15 g Protein; 730 mg Sodium*

# Tangy Pineapple Chicken

*If you are a fan of sweet and sour chicken, you'll love this dish. This delightfully tangy dish pairs perfectly with rice.*

| | | |
|---|---|---|
| Chopped onion | 1 cup | 250 mL |
| Sliced carrots | 1 cup | 250 mL |
| Sliced celery | 1 cup | 250 mL |
| Finely grated ginger root (or 1/2 tsp., 2 mL, ground ginger) | 2 tsp. | 10 mL |
| All-purpose flour | 1/4 cup | 60 mL |
| Curry powder | 2 tsp. | 10 mL |
| Salt | 1/2 tsp. | 2 mL |
| Pepper | 1/4 tsp. | 1 mL |
| Boneless, skinless chicken thighs (about 3 oz., 85 g, each) | 8 | 8 |
| Can of diced tomatoes (14 oz., 398 mL), with juice | 1 | 1 |
| Can of pineapple tidbits (14 oz., 398 mL), with juice | 1 | 1 |
| Ketchup | 1/4 cup | 60 mL |

Add first 4 ingredients to inner pot.

Combine next 4 ingredients in a large resealable freezer bag. Add chicken. Seal bag and toss until coated. Arrange chicken over vegetables. Sprinkle with any remaining flour mixture.

Combine remaining 3 ingredients in a medium bowl and pour over chicken. Cover with lid ensuring pressure release valve is in venting position. Select slow cooker function and cook on low for 5 to 6 hours or on high for 2 1/2 to 3 hours. Stir. Makes 4 servings.

*1 serving: 440 Calories; 11 g Total Fat (0 g Mono, 0 g Poly, 0 g Sat); 150 mg Cholesterol; 42 g Carbohydrate (5 g Fibre, 25 g Sugar); 44 g Protein; 970 mg Sodium*

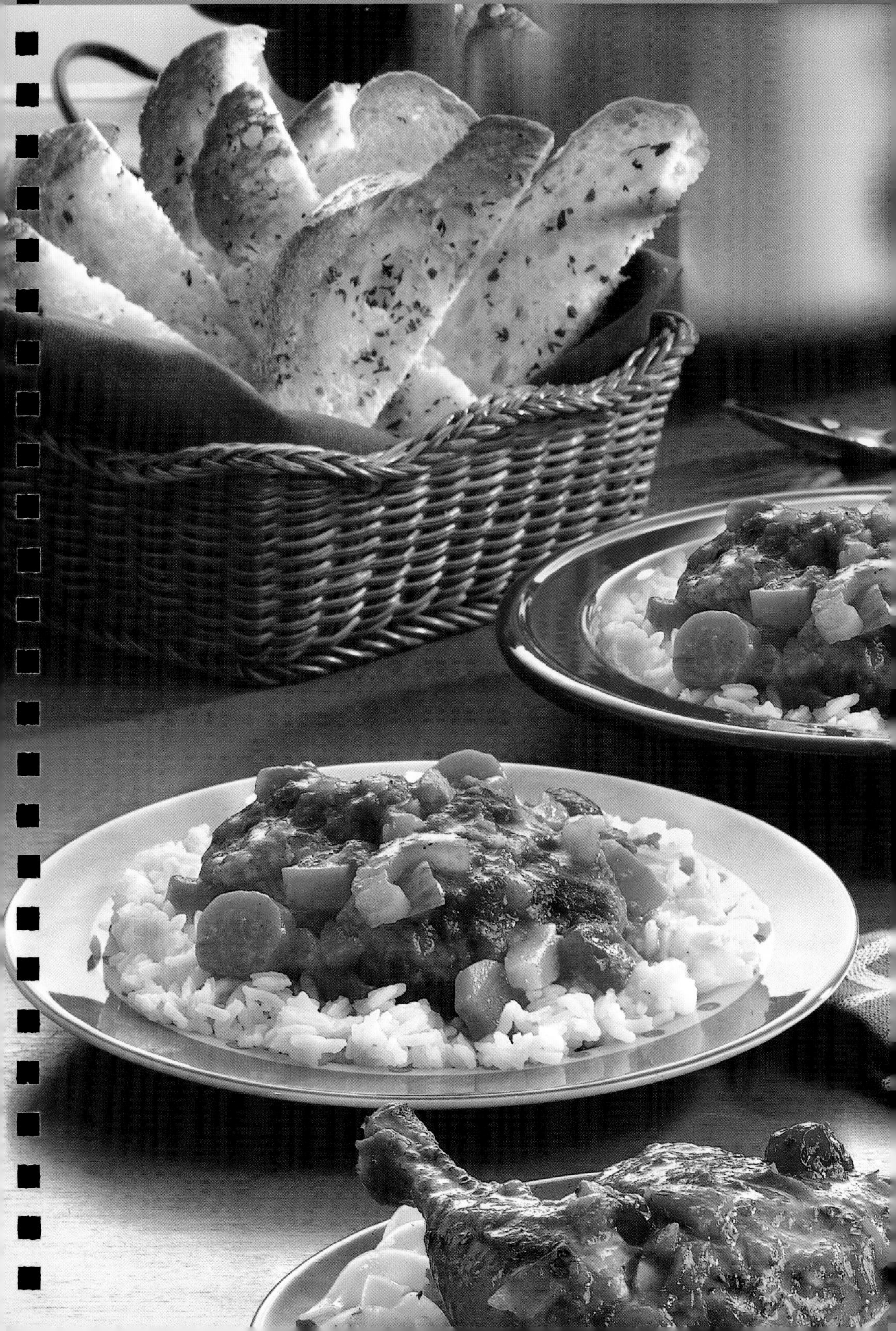

# Honey Garlic Wings

*These tender wings are a real crowd-pleaser with their classic honey garlic flavour. Set them out hot on a platter and watch everyone gather 'round.*

| | | |
|---|---|---|
| **Split chicken wings, tips discarded** | 3 lbs. | 1.4 kg |
| **Pepper, to taste** | | |
| **Liquid honey** | 1 cup | 250 mL |
| **Soy sauce** | 1/2 cup | 125 mL |
| **Garlic cloves, minced** | 2 | 2 |
| **(or 1/2 tsp., 2 mL, powder)** | | |
| **Ground ginger** | 1/4 tsp. | 1 mL |

Arrange wings on a greased baking sheet with sides. Sprinkle with pepper. Broil on top rack in oven for about 6 minutes per side until browned. Transfer to inner pot of multi-cooker.

Combine remaining 4 ingredients in a small bowl. Pour over chicken and stir until coated. Cover with lid ensuring pressure release valve is in venting position. Select slow cooker function and cook on low for 4 to 5 hours or on high for 2 to 2 1/2 hours. Discard liquid from inner pot. Makes about 32 wings.

*1 wing: 160 Calories; 9 g Total Fat (3.5 g Mono, 2 g Poly, 2.5 g Sat); 35 mg Cholesterol; 10 g Carbohydrate (0 g Fibre, 9 g Sugar); 12 g Protein; 250 mg Sodium*

# West Indian Chicken Curry

*The warm flavour of cinnamon and the sweetness of sugar work with the classic curry spices to make a delightful and satisfying chicken, potato and tomato dish.*

| | | |
|---|---|---|
| Cooking oil | 2 tbsp. | 30 mL |
| Chopped onion | 2 cups | 500 mL |
| Curry powder | 2 tbsp. | 30 mL |
| Brown sugar, packed | 1 tbsp. | 15 mL |
| Garlic cloves, minced | 2 | 2 |
| (or 1/2 tsp., 2 mL, powder) | | |
| Salt | 1/2 tsp. | 2 mL |
| Pepper | 1/2 tsp. | 2 mL |
| Ground cinnamon | 1/4 tsp. | 1 mL |
| Cayenne pepper | 1/8 tsp. | 0.5 mL |
| Boneless, skinless chicken breast halves, cut into 1 inch (2.5 cm) pieces | 1 lb. | 454 g |
| Can of diced tomatoes (14 oz., 398 mL), with juice | 1 | 1 |
| Baby potatoes, halved | 1/2 lb. | 225 g |
| Plain yogurt | 1/2 cup | 125 mL |

With sauté function, heat cooking oil in inner pot on medium. Add onion and cook for 3 minutes, stirring often. Stir in next 8 ingredients and cook for about 5 minutes, stirring occasionally, until chicken is browned.

Add tomatoes and potato. Heat, stirring and scraping any brown bits from bottom of pan, until boiling. Turn off sauté function. Cover with lid ensuring pressure release valve is in venting position. Select slow cooker function and cook on low for 5 to 7 hours or on high for 2 to 3 hours.

Stir in yogurt. Makes about 5 cups (1.25 L).

*1 cup (250 mL): 280 Calories; 8 g Total Fat (4 g Mono, 2 g Poly, 1 g Sat); 50 mg Cholesterol; 29 g Carbohydrate (4 g Fibre, 13 g Sugar); 25 g Protein; 450 mg Sodium*

# Slow Cooker Bouillabaisse

*This healthy take on a seafood favourite boasts a savoury broth rich with veggies, shrimp, fish and clams. Pairs perfectly with whole grain bread.*

| | | |
|---|---|---|
| Canola oil | 2 tsp. | 10 mL |
| Chopped onion | 2 cups | 500 mL |
| Chopped celery | 1 cup | 250 mL |
| Garlic cloves, minced (or 1/2 tsp., 2 mL, powder) | 2 | 2 |
| Can of diced tomatoes (28 oz., 796 mL), with juice | 1 | 1 |
| Chopped zucchini (with peel) | 3 cups | 750 mL |
| Prepared vegetable broth | 1 cup | 250 mL |
| Water | 1 cup | 250 mL |
| Dry (or alcohol-free) white wine | 1/2 cup | 125 mL |
| Tomato paste (see Tip, page 41) | 1/4 cup | 60 mL |
| Italian seasoning | 2 tsp. | 10 mL |
| Brown sugar, packed | 1/2 tsp. | 2 mL |
| Chili paste (sambal oelek) | 1/2 tsp. | 2 mL |
| Bay leaves | 2 | 2 |
| Haddock fillets, any small bones removed, cut into 1 inch (2.5 cm) pieces | 1 lb. | 454 g |
| Uncooked medium shrimp (peeled and deveined) | 3/4 lb. | 340 g |
| Can of whole baby clams (5 oz., 142 g), with liquid | 1 | 1 |

**Fresh basil leaves, for garnish**

With sauté function, heat canola oil in inner pot on medium. Add next 3 ingredients. Cook for about 10 minutes, stirring often, until celery is softened. Turn off sauté function.

Stir in next 10 ingredients. Cover with lid ensuring pressure release valve is in venting position. Select slow cooker function and cook on low for 8 to 9 hours or on high for 4 to 4 1/2 hours. Remove and discard bay leaves.

Add next 3 ingredients to inner pot and stir gently. Cook on high for about 30 minutes until fish flakes easily when tested with a fork.

Garnish with fresh basil. Makes about 12 1/2 cups (3.1 L).

*1 cup (250 mL): 130 Calories; 2 g Total Fat (.5 g Mono, .5 g Poly, 0 g Sat); 65 mg Cholesterol; 13 g Carbohydrate (2 g Fibre, 7 g Sugar); 15 g Protein; 400 mg Sodium*

# Spanish Chickpea Spinach Soup

*This thick, hearty soup is pleasantly flavoured with cumin and gets its texture from chickpeas and vegetables. It stores well in an airtight container in the freezer for up to three months.*

| | | |
|---|---|---|
| Cooking oil | 1 tbsp. | 15 mL |
| Chopped onion | 1 1/2 cups | 375 mL |
| Diced carrot | 1 cup | 250 mL |
| Diced peeled potato | 1 cup | 250 mL |
| Diced red pepper | 1 cup | 250 mL |
| Smoked (sweet) paprika | 1 1/2 tsp. | 7 mL |
| Ground cumin | 1 tsp. | 5 mL |
| Garlic cloves, minced | 2 | 2 |
| (or 1/2 tsp., 2 mL, powder) | | |
| Pepper | 1/2 tsp | 2 mL |
| Prepared vegetable broth | 4 cups | 1 L |
| Can of chickpeas (19 oz., 540 mL) | 1 | 1 |
| rinsed and drained | | |
| Bay leaf | 1 | 1 |
| Chopped fresh spinach leaves, | 2 cups | 500 mL |
| lightly packed | | |
| Chopped tomato | 1 cup | 250 mL |
| Red wine vinegar | 2 tbsp. | 30 mL |
| Granulated sugar | 1/2 tsp. | 2 mL |

With sauté function, heat cooking oil in inner pot on medium. Add onion and cook for about 8 minutes, stirring often, until softened.

Stir in next 7 ingredients and cook for about 3 minutes, stirring often, until garlic is fragrant.

Stir in next 3 ingredients, scraping any brown bits from bottom of pot. Turn off sauté function. Cover with lid ensuring pressure release valve is in venting position. Select slow cooker function and cook on low for 5 to 7 hours or on high for 2 to 3 hours. Remove and discard bay leaf.

Add remaining 4 ingredients. Heat, stirring, for about 2 minutes until spinach is wilted. Makes about 9 1/4 cups (2.3 L).

*1 cup (250 mL): 210 Calories; 4 g Total Fat (1.5 g Mono, 1.5 g Poly, .5 g Sat); 0 mg Cholesterol; 37 g Carbohydrate (8 g Fibre, 7 g Sugar); 13 g Protein; 160 mg Sodium*

# Dressed-up Dal

*Garnish individual servings with additional chopped tomato and fresh cilantro leaves, and serve with roti or naan bread.*

| | | |
|---|---|---|
| Cooking oil | 1 tbsp. | 15 mL |
| Chopped onion | 2 cups | 500 mL |
| Garlic cloves, minced (or 3/4 tsp., 4 mL, powder) | 3 | 3 |
| Curry powder | 2 tsp. | 10 mL |
| Cumin seed | 1 tsp. | 5 mL |
| Brown sugar, packed | 1 tsp. | 5 mL |
| Dried crushed chilies | 1/4 tsp. | 1 mL |
| Water | 6 cups | 1.5 L |
| Dried green lentils | 1 cup | 250 mL |
| Dried red split lentils | 1 cup | 250 mL |
| Cinnamon stick (4 inches, 10 cm) | 1 | 1 |
| Bay leaf | 1 | 1 |
| Chopped fresh spinach leaves, lightly packed | 3 cups | 750 mL |
| Chopped tomato | 1 cup | 250 mL |
| Chopped fresh cilantro (or parsley) | 1/4 cup | 60 mL |
| Lemon juice | 3 tbsp. | 45 mL |
| Finely grated ginger root (or 3/4 tsp., 4 mL, ground) | 1 tbsp. | 15 mL |
| Salt | 1/2 tsp. | 2 mL |

With sauté function, heat cooking oil in inner pot on medium. Add onion and cook for 5 minutes, stirring often, until onion starts to brown.

Add next 5 ingredients. Heat, stirring, for about 1 minute until fragrant. Turn off sauté function.

Stir in next 5 ingredients. Cover with lid ensuring pressure release valve is in venting position. Select slow cooker function and cook on low for 7 to 8 hours or on high for 3 1/2 to 4 hours.

Discard cinnamon stick and bay leaf. Add remaining 6 ingredients. Stir until spinach is wilted. Makes about 8 cups (2 L).

*1 cup (250 mL): 440 Calories; 2.5 g Total Fat (1 g Mono, 1 g Poly, 0 g Sat); 0 mg Cholesterol; 93 g Carbohydrate (7 g Fibre, 61 g Sugar); 16 g Protein; 160 mg Sodium*

# Sweet Potato and Bean Stew

*Soft sweet potatoes make the base for this flavourful stew and help to create a great texture that works perfectly with black beans and kidney beans.*

| | | |
|---|---|---|
| Chopped peeled orange-fleshed sweet potato | 4 cups | 1 L |
| Chopped onion | 1 cup | 250 mL |
| Can of white kidney beans (19 oz., 540 mL), rinsed and drained | 1 | 1 |
| Can of black beans (19 oz., 540 mL), rinsed and drained | 1 | 1 |
| Prepared vegetable broth | 1 cup | 250 mL |
| Chili powder | 2 tbsp. | 30 mL |
| Cocoa, sifted if lumpy | 1 tbsp. | 15 mL |
| Garlic powder | 1/2 tsp. | 2 mL |
| Salt | 1/4 tsp. | 1 mL |
| Pepper | 1/4 tsp. | 1 mL |
| Chopped tomato | 1 1/2 cups | 375 mL |
| Chopped fresh parsley | 2 tbsp. | 30 mL |

Layer first 4 ingredients, in order given, in inner pot.

Combine next 6 ingredients in a small bowl. Pour over beans. Do not stir. Cover with lid ensuring pressure release valve is in venting position. Select slow cooker function and cook on low for 7 to 8 hours or on High for 3 1/2 to 4 hours.

Stir in tomato and parsley. Makes about 6 1/2 cups (1.6 L).

*1 cup (250 mL):* 280 Calories; 2 g Total Fat (.5 g Mono, .5 g Poly, 0 g Sat); 0 mg Cholesterol; 55 g Carbohydrate (17 g Fibre, 9 g Sugar); 13 g Protein; 900 mg Sodium

# Slow Cooker Scallop

*Traditional scalloped potatoes are always welcome at a hearty feast. And because these are made in your multi-cooker, your oven will be free for any other dish your heart desires. Clean-up will be much easier if the inner pot is well greased for this recipe.*

| | | |
|---|---|---|
| Butter (or hard margarine) | 1/4 cup | 60 mL |
| All-purpose flour | 1/4 cup | 60 mL |
| Milk | 3 cups | 750 mL |
| Parsley flakes | 1 tbsp. | 15 mL |
| Dried rosemary, crushed | 1 tsp. | 5 mL |
| Garlic powder | 1/2 tsp. | 2 mL |
| Salt | 1 tsp. | 5 mL |
| Pepper | 1/2 tsp. | 2 mL |
| Peeled potatoes, thinly sliced | 5 lbs. | 2.3 kg |
| Thinly sliced onion | 2 cups | 500 mL |
| Grated Parmesan cheese | 1/4 cup | 60 mL |
| Paprika | 1/4 tsp. | 1 mL |

With sauté function, melt butter in well-greased inner pot on medium. Add flour. Heat, stirring, for 1 minute. Slowly add 1 cup (250 mL) milk, stirring constantly until boiling and thickened. Add remaining milk. Cook, stirring, until heated through. Turn off sauté function.

Stir in next 5 ingredients.

Add potato and onion and stir gently until well coated. Cover with lid ensuring pressure release valve is in venting position. Select slow cooker function and cook on low for 8 hours or on high for 4 hours.

Sprinkle with cheese and paprika. Let stand, covered, for 5 minutes. Makes 12 servings.

*1 serving: 250 Calories; 6 g Total Fat (1.5 g Mono, 0 g Poly, 3.5 g Sat); 15 mg Cholesterol; 41 g Carbohydrate (4 g Fibre, 6 g Sugar); 8 g Protein; 310 mg Sodium*

# Orange-Glazed Vegetables

*Everyone will love these tender carrots and sweet potatoes coated in a spiced orange glaze. Use orange-fleshed sweet potatoes for best results.*

| | | |
|---|---|---|
| **Baby carrots** | 1 lb. | 454 g |
| **Fresh, peeled orange-fleshed sweet potatoes, cut into 1 1/2 inch (3.8 cm) cubes** | 2 1/2 lbs. | 1.1 kg |
| **Chopped dried apricot** | 1 cup | 250 mL |
| **Maple (or maple-flavoured) syrup** | 1/2 cup | 125 mL |
| **Frozen concentrated orange juice** | 1/4 cup | 60 mL |
| **Water** | 1/4 cup | 60 mL |
| **Butter (or hard margarine), melted** | 2 tbsp. | 30 mL |
| **Salt** | 1/4 tsp. | 1 mL |
| **Pepper** | 1/4 tsp. | 1 mL |
| **Ground allspice** | 1/8 tsp. | 0.5 mL |
| **Water** | 1 tbsp. | 15 mL |
| **Cornstarch** | 2 tsp. | 10 mL |

Layer first 3 ingredients, in order given, in inner pot.

Combine next 7 ingredients in a small bowl. Pour over apricot. Cover with lid ensuring pressure release valve is in venting position. Select slow cooker function and cook on low for 6 hours or high for 3 hours. Transfer vegetables to a serving bowl with a slotted spoon.

With sauté function, bring liquid to a boil. Stir second amount of water into cornstarch in a small cup. Add to liquid. Heat, stirring, until boiling and thickened. Pour over vegetables. Makes 12 servings.

*1 serving: 140 Calories; 2.5 g Total Fat (.5 g Mono, 0 g Poly, 1.5 g Sat); 5 mg Cholesterol; 28 g Carbohydrate (3 g Fibre, 19 g Sugar); 4 g Protein; 95 mg Sodium*

# Maple Apple Bread Pudding

*This isn't your typical bread pudding; it is loaded with maple syrup, sweet bites of apple and the warm flavours of cinnamon and raisin. Delicious! Drizzle with extra maple syrup or caramel sauce, if you'd like.*

| | | |
|---|---|---|
| Large eggs | 4 | 4 |
| Can of 2 % evaporated milk (13 oz., 370 mL) | 1 | 1 |
| Milk | 1 cup | 250 mL |
| Brown sugar, packed | 1/4 cup | 60 mL |
| Maple syrup | 3 tbsp. | 45 mL |
| Vanilla extract | 1 tsp. | 5 mL |
| Ground cinnamon | 3/4 tsp. | 4 mL |
| Day-old white or multigrain bread cubes | 9 cups | 2.25 L |
| Chopped dried apple | 1 cup | 250 mL |
| Chopped golden raisins | 1/2 cup | 125 mL |

Whisk first 7 ingredients in greased inner pot.

Stir in remaining 3 ingredients. Cover with lid ensuring pressure release valve is in venting position. Select slow cooker function and cook on low for 3 to 3 1/2 hours until firm. Makes 8 servings.

*1 serving: 700 Calories; 11 g Total Fat (3 g Mono, 3 g Poly, 3.5 g Sat); 115 mg Cholesterol; 122 g Carbohydrate (7 g Fibre, 27 g Sugar); 26 g Protein; 1060 mg Sodium*

# Mango Blueberry Cobbler

*A whole wheat, cinnamon-spiced biscuit tops a sweet blueberry and mango filling for an aromatic cobbler with an inviting and cozy look.*

| | | |
|---|---|---|
| Chopped ripe (or frozen, thawed) mango | 5 cups | 1.25 L |
| Fresh (or frozen, thawed) blueberries | 4 cups | 1 L |
| Brown sugar, packed | 1/4 cup | 60 mL |
| All-purpose flour | 2 tbsp. | 30 mL |
| Grated lemon zest | 1/2 tsp. | 2 mL |
| All-purpose flour | 3/4 cup | 175 mL |
| Whole wheat flour | 1/2 cup | 125 mL |
| Brown sugar, packed | 1/4 cup | 60 mL |
| Baking powder | 2 tsp. | 10 mL |
| Ground cinnamon | 1/2 tsp. | 2 mL |
| Ground ginger | 1/2 tsp. | 2 mL |
| Salt | 1/8 tsp. | 0.5 mL |
| Milk | 2/3 cup | 150 mL |
| Canola oil | 2 tbsp. | 30 mL |
| Vanilla extract | 1 tsp. | 5 mL |

Combine first 5 ingredients in greased inner pot. Cover with lid ensuring pressure release valve is in venting position. Select slow cooker function and cook on low for 3 hours or on high for 1 to 1 1/2 hours. Stir.

Combine next 7 ingredients in a medium bowl. Make a well in centre.

Combine remaining 3 ingredients in a small bowl. Add to well and stir until just combined. Drop batter onto mango mixture, using about 1/4 cup (60 mL) for each mound. Cover with lid ensuring pressure release valve is in venting position and cook on high for about 2 to 2 1/2 hours until wooden pick inserted in centre of biscuit comes out clean. Makes 8 servings.

*1 serving:* 290 Calories; 4.5 g Total Fat (2.5 g Mono, 1.5 g Poly, .5 g Sat); 0 mg Cholesterol; 61 g Carbohydrate (5 g Fibre, 38 g Sugar); 4 g Protein; 50 mg Sodium

# The Rice Cooker

Most models of multi-cooker have two separate functions for cooking rice: rice and multigrain. The rice cooking function is meant exclusively for white rice, and the multigrain function is for brown rice, wild rice and other grains such as barley, bulgur and millet.

The shortcoming of the rice cooker function is that in many models it is not adjustable. Everyone has their own preference for how rice should be cooked, whether it is on the soft and wet side or more firm and dry. The rice cooking function cannot accommodate these preferences. The pressure cooking function, however, can. We have had consistently better results with the pressure cooking function than with the rice cooking preset, and we like the flexibility and greater control it offers us for our recipes.

On most multi-cookers, the multigrain function is adjustable so it can accommodate the different cooking times of various types of grains. Again, however, we've had better results with the pressure cooking function, and it takes less time to cook brown rice than using the multigrain function.

In the following recipes, we've provided instructions for both options, but we prefer to give the rice and multigrain functions a pass and use the pressure cooking function instead.

Whether you choose to use the pressure cooker function or the rice or multigrain presets, you should keep the following tips in mind.

• All types of rice, including wild rice, have the same water-to-rice ratio: 1:1. At first glance it might seem as though that amount of water is too low, but it works. Trust us. When you cook rice under pressure, it does not lose as much moisture as it does on the stove or in the oven, so you need less water to begin with.

• If you are using a liquid other than water to cook your rice, the ratio might be different.

• Always start with wet rice. Rinse your rice in a colander and shake off the excess water before adding it to the inner pot. If you skip this step, the 1:1 ratio does not work as well. The tiny amount of water that clings to the grains of rice provides just enough extra moisture to ensure your rice cooks properly.

• Because the multi-cooker needs at least 1 cup (250 mL) of water to work its magic, you should not cook less than 1 cup (250 mL) of rice at a time.

• The cooking time does not change according to the quantity of rice being cooked; it will be the same whether you are cooking 1 cup (250 mL) or 3 cups (750 mL). Brown rice takes about 25 minutes, white rice less than 10.

• Keep in mind that the cooking time and water-to-rice ratio are just starting points. Everyone has their own preference in rice, so adjust accordingly.

# Dolmades

*Serve these dolmades at room temperature or hot as a sit-down starter. You can find grape leaves in the international section of your local supermarket.*

| | | |
|---|---|---|
| **Finely chopped onion** | 1 1/2 cups | 375 mL |
| **Olive oil** | 2 tbsp. | 30 mL |
| **Chopped pine nuts (or pecans)** | 1/2 cup | 125 mL |
| **Basmati (or long grain white) rice, rinsed and drained** | 1 cup | 250 mL |
| **Water** | 1 cup | 250 mL |
| **Raisins** | 2/3 cup | 150 mL |
| **Parsley flakes (or 1/4 cup, 60 mL, chopped fresh)** | 1 tbsp. | 15 mL |
| **Salt** | 1 tsp. | 5 mL |
| **Pepper** | 1/8 tsp. | 0.5 mL |
| **Ground cinnamon** | 1/4 tsp. | 1 mL |
| **Seeded and chopped tomato** | 1 cup | 250 mL |
| **Jar of grape leaves (17 oz., 473 mL)** | 1 | 1 |
| **Lemon juice** | 1 1/2 tbsp. | 25 mL |
| **Olive oil** | 2 tbsp. | 30 mL |
| **Water** | 1 cup | 250 mL |

With sauté function, cook onion in first amount of olive oil over medium heat until soft.

Add pine nuts. Cook for 5 minutes until browned.

Stir in rice and first amount of water. Cover with lid and seal. Select rice cooker function (or pressure cooker function on high pressure for 6 minutes). Allow pressure to release naturally for 10 minutes, then do a quick release of remaining pressure.

Stir in raisins, parsley, salt, pepper, cinnamon and tomato. Transfer to a bowl and set aside until cool enough to handle. Wipe out inner pot and return to multi-cooker.

Rinse vine leaves under warm water. Drain and blot dry with a tea towel or paper towels. Place about 1 1/2 tbsp. (22 mL) rice mixture on each vine leaf. Roll stem end over rice, tucking in sides as you roll to completely enclose rice. Cover bottom and sides of inner pot with vine leaves. Arrange, seam side down, close together over leaves.

Sprinkle with lemon juice and second amount of olive oil. Cover surface with any remaining grape leaves. Add second amount of water. Cover with lid and seal. Cook with rice function. Allow pressure to release naturally for 10 minutes, then do a quick release of remaining pressure. Cool. Serve with a sprinkle of lemon juice. Makes 50 dolmades.

*1 dolmade:* 40 Calories; 2 g Total Fat (1 g Mono, .5 g Poly, 0 g Sat); 0 mg Cholesterol; 5 g Carbohydrate (1 g Fibre, 1 g Sugar); 1 g Protein; 60 mg Sodium

# Sweet Saffron Rice Pilaf

*Saffron can be a little expensive, but the aromatic flavour and intense colour it adds are worth every penny. Nuts and fruit add flavour to this golden rice dish.*

| | | |
|---|---|---|
| Warm water | 1 tbsp. | 15 mL |
| Saffron threads | 1/4 tsp. | 1 mL |
| Butter (or hard margarine) | 2 tbsp. | 30 mL |
| Finely chopped onion | 1/2 cup | 125 mL |
| Chopped pistachios | 1/2 cup | 125 mL |
| Chopped dried apricot | 1/4 cup | 60 mL |
| Dried cranberries | 1/4 cup | 60 mL |
| Liquid honey | 1/4 cup | 60 mL |
| Grated orange zest | 1 tbsp. | 15 mL |
| Water | 1 1/2 cups | 375 mL |
| White basmati (or long-grain) rice | 1 1/2 cups | 375 mL |
| Salt | 3/4 tsp. | 4 mL |

Combine warm water and saffron in a small bowl. Set aside.

With sauté function, heat butter in inner pot on medium. Add onion and cook for about 5 minutes, stirring often, until softened.

Add next 5 ingredients and saffron mixture. Cook, stirring, for 1 minute. Turn off sauté function.

Stir in rice, water and salt. Cover with lid and seal. Select rice function (or pressure cooker function on high pressure and cook for 6 minutes). Allow pressure to release naturally for 10 minutes and then do a quick release of any remaining pressure. Makes about 6 cups (1.3 L).

*1 cup (250 mL):* 340 Calories; 0 g Total Fat (3.5 g Mono, 1.5 g Poly, 3 g Sat); 10 mg Cholesterol; 62 g Carbohydrate (2 g Fibre, 17 g Sugar); 7 g Protein; 390 mg Sodium

# Italian Barley Pilaf

*This colourful side dish is the perfect accompaniment for grilled or roasted meat or fish.*

| | | |
|---|---|---|
| **Water** | 3 cups | 750 mL |
| **Pot barley** | 1 cup | 250 mL |
| **Olive oil** | 1 tbsp. | 15 mL |
| **Finely chopped carrot** | 1 cup | 250 mL |
| **Finely chopped onion** | 1 cup | 250 mL |
| **Finely chopped zucchini (with peel)** | 1 cup | 250 mL |
| **Dried oregano** | 1/2 tsp. | 2 mL |
| **Salt** | 1/2 tsp. | 2 mL |
| **Pepper** | 1/8 tsp. | 0.5 mL |
| **Diced seeded tomato** | 1 cup | 250 mL |
| **Chopped fresh basil** | 2 tbsp. | 30 mL |
| **White wine vinegar** | 1 tsp. | 5 mL |

Combine water and barley in inner pot. Cover with lid and seal. Select multigrain function (or pressure cooker function on high pressure) and cook for 22 minutes. Remove barley from pot and set aside, covered, to keep warm.

Wipe out inner pot, and with sauté function, heat olive oil on medium. Add next 6 ingredients. Cook for about 10 minutes, stirring often, until vegetables are softened.

Stir in remaining 3 ingredients and barley. Makes about 5 1/2 cups (1.4 L).

*1/2 cup (125 mL): 80 Calories; 1.5 g Total Fat (1 g Mono, 0 g Poly, 0 g Sat); 0 mg Cholesterol; 15 g Carbohydrate (3 g Fibre, 2 g Sugar); 2 g Protein; 95 mg Sodium*

# Brown Rice Pilaf

*Many people shy away from brown rice because of its reputation for being finicky to cook, but with the multi-cooker, it couldn't be easier. The combination of mushroom, brown rice and Parmesan in this dish is irresistible. Serve with a fresh spinach salad.*

| | | |
|---|---|---|
| **Olive (or canola) oil** | 1 tbsp. | 15 mL |
| **Finely chopped onion** | 1 cup | 250 mL |
| **Sliced mushrooms** | 1 cup | 250 mL |
| **Long grain brown rice** | 1 cup | 250 mL |
| **Prepared chicken or vegetable broth** | 1 cup | 250 mL |
| **Finely chopped spinach** | 1/4 cup | 60 mL |
| **Lemon wedges (optional)** | 4 | 4 |
| **Grated Parmesan cheese** | 1/4 cup | 60 mL |

With sauté function, heat olive oil in inner pot on medium. Add onion and mushroom and cook for 5 to 10 minutes, stirring often, until onion is softened.

Add rice and stir until coated. Stir in broth. Cover with lid and seal. Select multigrain function (or pressure cooker function on high pressure) and cook for 25 minutes. Allow pressure to release naturally for 10 minutes and then do a quick release of the remaining pressure.

Stir in spinach. Divide amongst 4 plates or bowls, and squeeze 1 lemon wedge over each serving, if using. Sprinkle with Parmesan. Makes 4 servings.

*1 cup (250 mL):* 270 Calories; 4.5 g Total Fat (2 g Mono, 1 g Poly, .5 g Sat); 0 mg Cholesterol; 52 g Carbohydrate (4 g Fibre, 8 g Sugar); 8 g Protein; 310 mg Sodium

# Nutty Mushroom Wild Rice

*The lovely contrasting textures of chewy brown and wild rice and crunchy nuts make for a flavourful side dish that is excellent with fish or chicken.*

| | | |
|---|---|---|
| Prepared chicken broth | 2 1/4 cups | 550 mL |
| Brown rice | 2/3 cup | 150 mL |
| Wild rice | 1/3 cup | 75 mL |
| Butter (or hard margarine) | 1 tbsp. | 15 mL |
| Sliced fresh white mushrooms | 2 cups | 500 mL |
| Finely chopped onion | 1/3 cup | 75 mL |
| Pine nuts, toasted (see Tip, page 72) | 2 tbsp. | 30 mL |
| Slivered almonds, toasted (see Tip, page 72) | 2 tbsp. | 30 mL |
| Pepper | 1/4 tsp. | 1 mL |

With sauté function, melt butter in inner pot on medium. Add mushrooms and onion and cook for 10 to 15 minutes, stirring often, until mushrooms are browned. Turn off sauté function.

Add broth, brown rice and wild rice to inner pot. Cover with lid and seal. Select multigrain function (or pressure cooker function on high pressure) and cook for 27 minutes. Allow pressure to release naturally for 10 minutes and then do a quick release of remaining pressure. Transfer to a medium bowl.

Stir in remaining 3 ingredients. Makes 4 servings.

*1 serving:* 150 Calories; 8 g Total Fat (3 g Mono, 2.5 g Poly, 2.5 g Sat); 10 mg Cholesterol; 14 g Carbohydrate (2 g Fibre, 2 g Sugar); 7 g Protein; 350 mg Sodium

# Bulgur Chickpea Curry

*Chickpea curries are a tasty staple at Indo-Asian restaurants. We've added nutty bulgur for a one-two punch of nutritious grains and legumes. Serve with pork or lamb stew, fish or grilled chicken.*

| | | |
|---|---|---|
| Cooking oil | 1 tsp. | 5 mL |
| Chopped onion | 1 cup | 250 mL |
| Garlic cloves, minced | 2 | 2 |
| (or 1/2 tsp., 2 mL, powder) | | |
| Finely chopped red pepper | 1 cup | 250 mL |
| Bulgur | 3/4 cup | 175 mL |
| Can of chickpeas (19 oz., 540 mL), | 1 | 1 |
| rinsed and drained | | |
| Prepared vegetable broth | 1 1/4 cups | 300 mL |
| Curry powder | 1 tsp. | 5 mL |
| Ground cinnamon | 1/4 tsp. | 1 mL |
| Ground cumin | 1/4 tsp. | 1 mL |
| Salt | 1/2 tsp. | 2 mL |
| Pepper | 1/4 tsp. | 1 mL |

With sauté function, heat cooking oil in inner pot on medium. Add onion and garlic and cook for 5 to 10 minutes, stirring occasionally, until onion is softened.

Add red pepper and cook until tender-crisp. Add bulgur and stir until well coated with oil. Turn off sauté function.

Add remaining 7 ingredients. Cover with lid and seal. Select rice cooker function (or pressure cooker function on high) and cook for 12 minutes. Makes about 5 cups (1.25 L).

*1 cup (250 mL):* 440 Calories; 7 g Total Fat (2 g Mono, 3 g Poly, .5 g Sat); 0 mg Cholesterol; 77 g Carbohydrate (12 g Fibre, 13 g Sugar); 21 g Protein; 290 mg Sodium

# The Steamer

Steaming food in the multi-cooker is not the same as steaming food over a pot of boiling water on your stovetop. With the multi-cooker's steamer function, the food is cooked under pressure. This means that the food cooks much faster than it would on the stove. However, as with all pressure cooking, you need to factor in the time it takes for the pressure to build before the steaming process begins.

Not all foods were meant to be steamed in the multi-cooker. If you love a plate of crisp, steamed broccoli, use the stovetop method instead. In the multi-cooker, the food begins cooking as the pressure builds, before the actual cooking time even begins. Even with the timer set to zero and a quick release of pressure, broccoli tends to come out limp and over-cooked. The same can be said for most delicate vegetables, including leafy greens, such as spinach. Use the steamer function for root vegetables such as beets, potatoes and yams, as well as corn on the cob. Artichokes also come out perfectly cooked, though they can be a little difficult to find out of season, depending on where you live.

Delicate fish and seafood are also iffy choices for the multi-cooker's steamer function. Whereas hardier selections like lobster, crab and salmon can fare well when steamed under pressure, you are better off cooking shrimp, scallops or mussels on your stovetop or barbeque to avoid disappointment.

When you are using the steamer function, make sure no food touches the bottom of the inner pot. To generate enough steam for cooking, the multi-cooker uses extreme heat to bring the water at the bottom of the pot to a boil quickly, and any food touching the bottom of the pot is likely to burn under such intense heat. The trivet that comes with your multi-cooker can be used as a steaming tray to elevate your food above the water when you are cooking large items. However, if you are cooking chopped veggies or other small items, you will have a much easier time getting them out of the inner pot if you use a steamer basket. Metal or silicone steamer baskets both work well. Just place the basket on the trivet to keep the food well away from the water in the bottom of the pot.

We recommend a quick release of the pressure for all foods you are steaming. Allowing the pressure to release naturally adds cooking time to the dish (the food continues to cook while the pressure dissipates) and can result in over-cooked food.

# Thai Peanut Sweet Potatoes

*A mildly spicy peanut sauce coats tender sweet potatoes in this simple side that makes a great accompaniment to chicken or pork.*

| | | |
|---|---|---|
| Cubed fresh peeled sweet potato | 4 cups | 1 L |
| Water | 1 cup | 250 mL |
| Cooking oil | 1 tbsp. | 15 mL |
| Chopped onion | 1 cup | 250 mL |
| Garlic cloves, minced (or 1/2 tsp., 2 mL, powder) | 2 | 2 |
| Finely grated ginger root | 1 tsp. | 5 mL |
| Thai peanut sauce | 3 tbsp. | 45 mL |

Place trivet in inner pot and add water. Place sweet potato in a metal or silicone steamer basket and lower into inner pot. Cover with lid and seal. Select steamer function and cook for 2 minutes. Do a quick release of pressure. Transfer potatoes to a large bowl and cover to keep warm. Drain water from inner pot.

With sauté function, heat cooking oil in inner pot on medium. Add onion and cook for about 5 minutes, stirring occasionally, until softened.

Add garlic and ginger. Cook, stirring, for about 1 minute, until fragrant.

Stir in peanut sauce. Add sweet potato and cook until warmed through, about 3 minutes. Makes about 3 cups.

*1/2 cup (125 mL): 120 Calories; 1.5 g Total Fat (0 g Mono, 0 g Poly, 0 g Sat); 0 mg Cholesterol; 25 g Carbohydrate (4 g Fibre, 7 g Sugar); 3 g Protein; 410 mg Sodium*

# Corn on the Cob with Honey Herb Butter

*Gone are the days of heating up your kitchen with huge pot of boiling water bubbling away on the stovetop just to cook a few cobs of corn. With the multi-cooker, cooking corn on the cob is quick and easy, and the corn comes out crisp and delicious.*

| | | |
|---|---|---|
| Butter, room temperature | 4 oz. | 125 g |
| Honey | 1 tbsp. | 15 mL |
| Chopped herbs, such as parsley or thyme | 1 tsp. | 5 mL |
| Salt, to taste | | |
| Pepper, to taste | | |
| | | |
| Water | 1 cup | 250 mL |
| Corncobs | 4 | 4 |

For the butter, combine first 5 ingredients in a medium bowl and mix well to combine. Set aside.

Place trivet in inner pot and add water. Add corn. Cover with lid and seal. Select steamer function and cook for 2 minutes. Do a quick release of pressure. Serve with herb butter. Makes 4 servings.

*1 cob with 1 tbsp. (15 mL) butter: 180 Calories; 11 g Total Fat (2.5 g Mono, 0 g Poly, 6 g Sat); 25 mg Cholesterol; 21 g Carbohydrate (2 g Fibre, 4 g Sugar); 3 g Protein; 15 mg Sodium*

# Chili Cheese Potatoes

*The heat of chili paste and the saltiness of Parmesan give depth and robust flavour to perfectly cooked baby potatoes.*

| | | |
|---|---|---|
| Baby potatoes, quartered | 2 lbs. | 900 g |
| Water | 1 cup | 250 mL |
| Cooking oil | 2 tbsp. | 30 mL |
| Chili paste (sambal oelek) | 2 tsp. | 10 mL |
| Salt | 1/2 tsp. | 2 mL |
| Grated Parmesan cheese | 1/2 cup | 125 mL |
| Crumbled cooked bacon | 1/4 cup | 60 mL |
| Chopped parsley | 2 tbsp. | 30 mL |

Place trivet in inner pot and add water. Place potato in a metal or silicone steamer basket and lower into inner pot. Cover with lid and seal. Select steamer function and cook for 2 minutes. Do a quick release of the pressure.

Whisk next 3 ingredients in a medium bowl. Add potato and toss to coat.

Sprinkle with cheese, bacon and parsley. Makes about 2 1/2 cups (625 mL).

*1/2 cup (125 mL):* 120 Calories; 4.5 g Total Fat (2 g Mono, 1 g Poly, 1 g Sat); 0 mg Cholesterol; 16 g Carbohydrate (1 g Fibre, 0 g Sugar); 4 g Protein; 190 mg Sodium

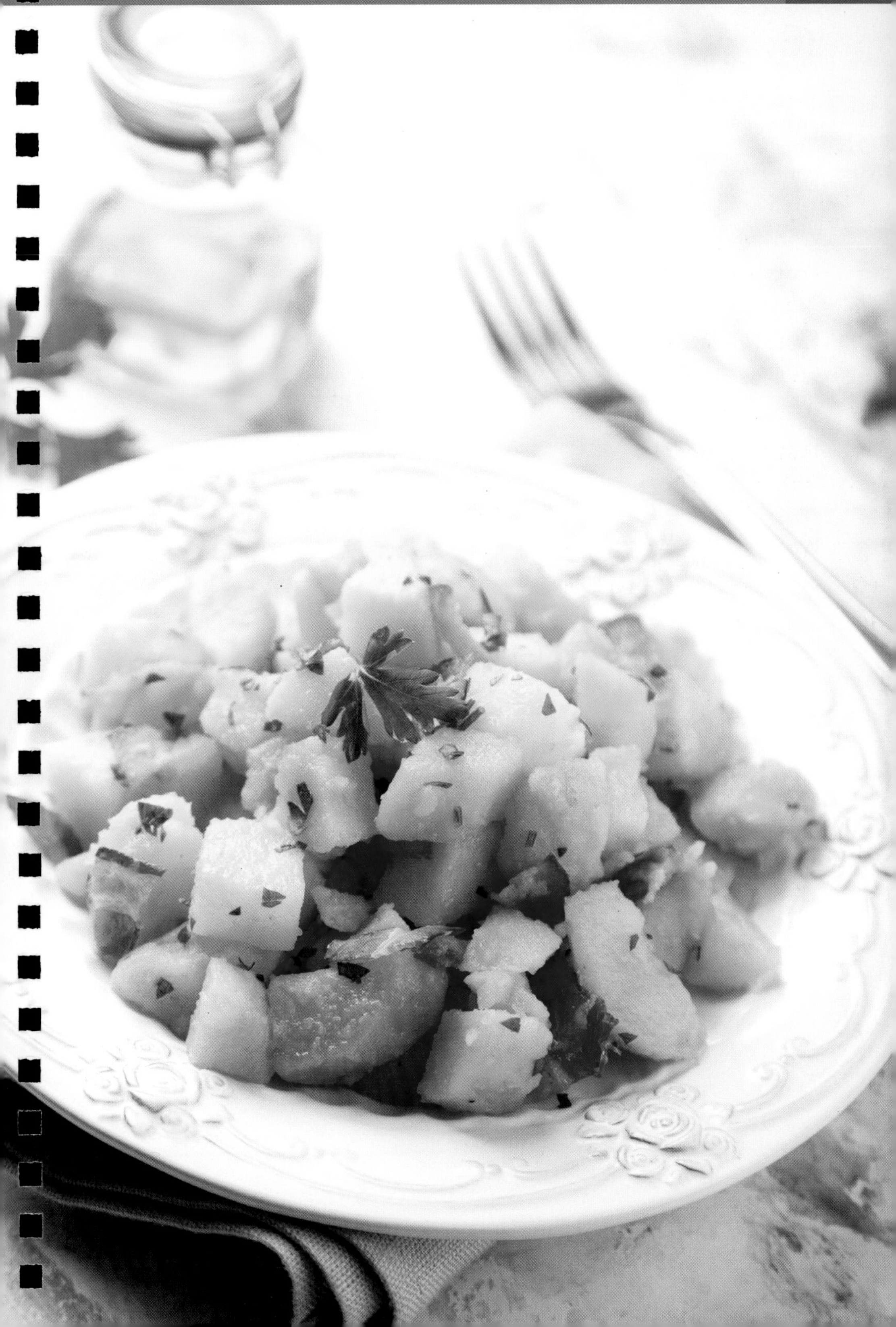

# Basil Honey Asparagus

*These tender asparagus spears are lightly dressed in a subtly sweet and tangy basil vinaigrette. A simple yet superb side.*

| | | |
|---|---|---|
| Water | 1 cup | 250 mL |
| Fresh asparagus, trimmed of tough ends | 1 lb. | 454 g |
| Olive (or cooking) oil | 1/4 cup | 60 mL |
| Apple cider vinegar | 2 tbsp. | 30 mL |
| Chopped fresh basil (or 1 1/2 tsp., 7 mL, dried) | 1 tbsp. | 15 mL |
| Grated Parmesan cheese | 1 tbsp. | 15 mL |
| Liquid honey | 1 tbsp. | 15 mL |
| Dry mustard | 1 tsp. | 5 mL |
| Salt | 1/8 tsp. | 0.5 mL |

Place trivet in inner pot. Add water and bring to a boil with sauté function. Place asparagus in a steaming basket and set inside inner pot. Close lid and seal. Select steamer function and cook for 2 minutes (1 if spears are very thin). Do a quick release of pressure. Transfer spears to a serving plate.

Combine remaining 7 ingredients in jar with a tight-fitting lid. Shake well. Makes about 1/2 cup (125 mL) vinaigrette. Drizzle over asparagus. Makes 4 servings.

*1 serving: 150 Calories; 14 g Total Fat (10 g Mono, 1.5 g Poly, 2 g Sat); 0 mg Cholesterol; 5 g Carbohydrate (2 g Fibre, 3 g Sugar); 3 g Protein; 25 mg Sodium*

# Honeyed Carrots

*These tender carrots with their sweet glaze will please the whole family. If you like your carrots firmer, stop the steamer cycle after 30 seconds of cooking time.*

| | | |
|---|---|---|
| **Medium carrots, cut in half and then quartered (about 10 carrots)** | **2 lbs.** | **900 g** |
| **Water** | **1 cup** | **250 mL** |
| **Liquid honey** | **2 tbsp.** | **30 mL** |
| **Ground cinnamon, sprinkle** | | |
| **Salt** | **1/2 tsp.** | **2 mL** |

Place trivet in inner pot and add water. Place carrots in a metal or silicone steamer basket and lower into inner pot. Cover with lid and seal. Select steamer function and cook for 1 minute. Do a quick release of pressure. Remove steamer basket and drain water from inner pot. Pour carrot back into inner pot.

Drizzle honey over carrot. Sprinkle with cinnamon and salt. With sauté function, cook on medium for 5 to 6 minutes, stirring constantly, until carrot is glazed and liquid has evaporated. Makes 4 cups (1 L).

*1/2 cup (125 mL): 40 Calories; 0 g Total Fat (0 g Mono, 0 g Poly, 0 g Sat); 0 mg Cholesterol; 10 g Carbohydrate (1 g Fibre, 7 g Sugar); 1 g Protein; 160 mg Sodium*

# Yogurt Maker

Yogurt making is a slow, lengthy process, but with your multi-cooker, it is painless. Most of the time involved is inactive time, meaning you can just go about your usual business as your trusty multi-cooker does its thing and produces some of the creamiest yogurt you will ever taste.

Making yogurt in your multi-cooker is a 4-step process:

1. First you need to heat 8 cups (2 L) of milk to 180°F (82°C) to denature the proteins and kill off any bacteria that might interfere with the "good" bacteria you will be adding with your starter.

Use the yogurt function to heat the milk to the appropriate temperature. If your multi-cooker does not have a yogurt function, you can use the sauté function for this step, though you'll have to stir the milk frequently to prevent it from scorching, or use the keep warm function to heat the milk more slowly.

2. Once the heating step is complete, allow the milk to cool to 110°F (43°C). When you remove the multi-cooker's lid, make sure the moisture that accumulated in the lid during the heating process does not drip into the milk. You can leave the milk in the multi-cooker to cool, but it will cool much quicker if you move the inner pot out of the cooker and set it on a rack or trivet on the counter.

3. When your milk is cool enough, add the starter. Don't be tempted to rush this step: If the milk is warmer than 110°F (43°C), it will kill the "good" bacteria in your starter. Add 2 tbsp. (30 mL) of your yogurt of choice to the cooled milk and stir well. Make sure the yogurt you choose for your starter has a live, active bacteria culture or your milk will not ferment into yogurt.

4. This next step takes the longest amount of time but does not involve any labour on your part except placing the inner pot back into the multi-cooker, putting on the lid and sealing it, and then pushing the yogurt function and adjusting the time setting. Your mixture must incubate for about 8 hours at 97 to 109°F (36 to 42°C) so that the active bacteria can work its magic and turn the milk mixture into yogurt. If your multi-cooker does not have a yogurt function, wrap the multi-cooker with a few thick towels or a blanket to keep in the heat and then let it sit.

When you open the lid at the end of the cycle, you'll have a layer of thin, watery liquid on top of your yogurt. This liquid is whey that has separated from the milk during the cooking process. You can either stir it back into the yogurt, or if you'd like a thicker yogurt, pour it off or strain the yogurt through some cheesecloth or a coffee filter.

## Yogurt-making Tips:

• An instant-read thermometer is a must-have for yogurt-making. If your milk is not at the correct temperature for the heating and cooling stages, your yogurt might not turn out.

• The longer your yogurt incubates, the tangier or more sour it becomes. If you like your yogurt on the sour side, increase the incubation time to about 10 hours.

• Experiment with different types of milk. Homogenized or 2 percent milk will produce a thick, creamy yogurt; skim milk will produce a much thinner yogurt. You can also use sheep, goat or even plant-based milks, such as almond or coconut milk, but you'll need a special starter for the plant-based milks.

• When choosing your starter, use a plain yogurt with no additives or thickeners, such as cornstarch or gelatin. Additives can interfere with the bacteria's ability to ferment the milk and will affect the quality of your yogurt.

• Different commercial brands of yogurt use different strains of bacteria in their product, and each strain of bacteria produces a yogurt with a slightly different flavour. Try different brands until you find the one that produces a finished product that best suits your taste.

• You can use a previous batch of homemade yogurt as a starter, but after a few batches you will notice that your yogurt is not setting properly. This is a sign that you need a new starter and should add a container of yogurt to your next grocery list.

• If you want to add flavouring, fruit or sweeteners to your yogurt, do so after the incubation period is complete. They can interfere with the bacteria's ability to ferment the milk.

# Frozen Berry Soufflés

*Use your homemade yogurt to make this impressive frozen dessert that looks just like a baked soufflé.*

| | | |
|---|---|---|
| **Box of raspberry jelly powder (gelatin) (3 oz., 85 g)** | 1 | 1 |
| **Boiling water** | 1 cup | 250 mL |
| **Frozen mixed berries** | 1 1/2 cups | 375 mL |
| **Homemade yogurt** | 1/2 cup | 125 mL |
| **Whipping cream** | 1/2 cup | 125 mL |
| **Fresh raspberries, for garnish** | 1/2 cup | 125 mL |

Cut 4 strips of parchment paper about 3 inches (7.5 cm) wide and long enough to fit outside circumference of 3/4 cup (175 mL) ramekins. Secure with tape and set aside. Stir jelly powder into boiling water in a medium heatproof bowl until jelly powder is dissolved.

Add berries. Stir until mixture starts to thicken. Stir in yogurt and chill for about 20 minutes until mixture starts to set.

Beat whipping cream in a small bowl until stiff peaks form. Fold in berry mixture. Spoon into prepared ramekins. Freeze for about 2 hours until set. Remove parchment paper.

Garnish with raspberries. Makes 4 soufflés.

*1 soufflé: 240 Calories; 10 g Total Fat (3 g Mono, .5 g Poly, 6 g Sat); 35 mg Cholesterol; 34 g Carbohydrate (4 g Fibre, 29 g Sugar); 5 g Protein; 135 mg Sodium*

# Index by Function

# Recipe Index